WAIT *and* HOPE

Wait and Hope
© 2024 by Jacob Tanner

All rights reserved. No part of this book may be used or reproduced in any manner whatsoever without written permission except in the case of brief quotations embodied in critical articles and reviews. Direct your requests to the publisher at the following addresses:

Reformation Heritage Books
3070 29th St. SE
Grand Rapids, MI 49512
616-977-0889
orders@heritagebooks.org
www.heritagebooks.org

Scripture taken from the King James Version. In the public domain.

Printed in the United States of America
24 25 26 27 28 29/10 9 8 7 6 5 4 3 2 1

Library of Congress Cataloging-in-Publication Data

Names: Tanner, Jacob J., Jr. author.
Title: Wait and hope : Puritan wisdom for joyful suffering / Jacob Tanner.
Description: Grand Rapids, Michigan : Reformation Heritage Books, [2024] | Includes bibliographical references.
Identifiers: LCCN 2024014886 (print) | LCCN 2024014887 (ebook) | ISBN 9798886861174 (paperback) | ISBN 9798886861181 (epub)
Subjects: LCSH: Puritans—History. | Puritans—Study and teaching. | Bible—Study and teaching. | Hop—Religious aspects—Christianity.
Classification: LCC BX9323 .T64 2024 (print) | LCC BX9323 (ebook) | DDC 285/.9—dc23/eng/20240520
LC record available at https://lccn.loc.gov/2024014886
LC ebook record available at https://lccn.loc.gov/2024014887

Dedication

For my dad,
GLENN TANNER SR.
whose confidence in the face of suffering and death
encapsulated the wisdom of "wait and hope"

"For our light affliction, which is but for a moment, worketh for us a far more exceeding and eternal weight of glory; while we look not at the things which are seen, but at the things which are not seen: for the things which are seen are temporal; but the things which are not seen are eternal." (2 Cor. 4:17–18)

Enjoy this eternal weight of glory
until we meet again before Jesus's throne.

Contents

Introduction ix

1. The Trial and Triumph of Mortifying the Flesh 1
2. Fighting for Faith and Assurance When Battling Unbelief ... 19
3. Remembering God's Sovereignty When the World Spins Out of Control 35
4. Following the One Who Endured the Cross, Despising Its Shame..................................... 51
5. Passionately Living for Christ under Persecution.......... 65
6. Living as Outcasts, Vagabonds, and Pilgrims with Joy 81
7. Clinging to God's Promises in Sickness 95
8. When Death Calls Us Home 109
9. When Weeping Tarries for the Night 125
10. Joy Comes in the Morning............................. 139

Conclusion: The Puritan Hope of Triumph in the Midst of Suffering 155
Bibliography 165

Introduction

The Count of Monte Cristo is a bona fide literary classic for a reason. Published as a serial from 1844 to 1846, the story is expertly crafted by Alexandre Dumas, who takes readers on a magnificently woven and astonishing journey that explores the depths of human depravity and the heights of God's beauties and graces that make up mankind's life experiences. In a little over a thousand pages, Dumas pens a tale of betrayal, revenge, retribution, and revival. In lesser hands, the tale would be a thoroughly dark one, exhausting in its scope, and devoid of any goodness or beauty. But in Dumas's capable hands, the story becomes one primarily of *hope*.

Perhaps the most famous lines from the novel appear near the end. After readers have been taken on a thrilling adventure of incredible twists and turns, Dumas writes these profound words: "Live, then, and be happy, beloved children of my heart, and never forget, that until the day God will deign to reveal the future to man, all human wisdom is contained in these two words, 'Wait and Hope.'"[1]

These are simple words, yes, but they are profound. Human experience as a whole, and especially Christian experience, attests to the validity of these two words. We often find ourselves in a state of both *waiting* and *hoping*. Sometimes we are waiting on a message of one sort or another, hoping for good news to be delivered. Sometimes we are waiting for a particular day, like a wedding or the birth of a child,

---

1. Alexandre Dumas, *The Count of Monte Cristo*, trans. Robin Buss (New York: Penguin Books, 1996), 1243.

hoping that the day is all we long for it to be. Sometimes we are waiting for somebody to come to us, hoping that they bring with them something we need. Sometimes we are waiting for suffering to pass, hoping that the Lord will soon deliver us from evil. Whatever we wait for, as Dumas wrote, we wait with hope until the Lord should choose to make all things known.

Waiting and Hoping with the Puritans
If we wish to learn how to wait and hope in such a way that God would be glorified, even through our suffering, then we must look to the testimony of Scripture and the lives of past saints. We must remember that we stand on the shoulders of those who came before us, and if we ignore church history, we do so to our own peril. Strong saints are often well read in church history. And when it comes to enduring suffering and hoping in the triumph of Christ, perhaps there is no better place to turn to in the pages of church history than the lives and teachings of the Puritans.

The Puritan age is typically regarded as having occurred during the seventeenth century. These were the men and women who, picking up the mantle of the Reformers in the century prior, continued the business of reforming the church for the glory of God. Men like John Owen, John Bunyan, Thomas Brooks, Richard Sibbes, and Nehemiah Coxe strove to see the church (and especially the Church of England) purified through reform. Their beliefs often landed them in hot water with the culture of their day, with many enemies surrounding them both within and without their churches. They suffered immensely for Christ and yet hoped for the triumphant victory that they had been promised through faith in Him.

Yes, the Puritans understood this paradigm of waiting and hoping quite well. As they waited for the day when all things would be placed under the feet of Jesus (Ps. 110:1; Luke 20:42–43; Acts 2:34–35; 1 Cor. 15:25; Heb. 1:13; 10:13), they hoped that the kingdom of God would continue to advance and their earthly suffering, by God's grace, would cease. They had a profound hope in the triumph of Christ and His church over everything. This triumphant hope colored all their activities. For the Puritans, the Christian life was not an idle life, but a militant life because of Christ's—and the church's—ultimate triumph.

Iain Murray, in his exquisite *The Puritan Hope*, wrote about this very thing. Quoting first from J. C. Ryle in his introduction, he explains how the Puritans became influential for the generations of Christendom that followed:

> J. C. Ryle in "An Estimate of Thomas Manton" written in 1870 says, "The Puritans, as a body, have done more to elevate the national character than any class of English men that ever lived." The source of this influence was their theology and within that theology there was an attitude to history and to the world which distinguished them as men of hope. In their own day this hope came to expression in pulpits and in books, in Parliaments and upon battlefields, but it did not end there. The outlook they had done so much to inspire went on for nearly two hundred years after their own age and its results were manifold. It coloured the spiritual thought of the American colonies; it taught men to expect great outpouring of the Holy Spirit; it prepared the way to the new age of world-missions; and it contributed largely to that sense of destiny which came to characterize the English-speaking Protestant nations. When nineteenth-century Christian leaders such as William Wilberforce viewed the world not as much as a wreck from which individual souls must escape, but rather as the property of Christ, to whose kingdom the earth and the fulness thereof must belong, their thinking bore the genuine hall-mark of the Puritan outlook.[2]

The Puritans were not daydreamers with their heads in the clouds or credulous in their hopes for the future. They were not mere optimists or naive in their trust in God's promises. They were men and women of faith. Choosing to live by faith in what God had promised in His Word, rather than by what their eyes saw and senses told them, meant that a steady hope for the future had been engraved into their consciences. As followers of Christ, they could have sooner sprouted

---

2. Iain H. Murray, *The Puritan Hope: A Study in Revival and the Interpretation of Prophecy* (Edinburgh: Banner of Truth, 1971), xxi–xxii.

wings to fly than abandon the hope they had discovered in the gospel. And it was this hope that influenced and informed every aspect of their lives.

They were not ignorant of the troubles surrounding them or blind to the issues they faced. On the contrary, they saw the wickedness in the world around them just as clearly as you and I see these things today. They were not fools who denied what their senses taught them. They knew things were bad. Yet they waited, they hoped, they were of good cheer.

Most importantly, the Puritans were not ivory-tower navel gazers who thought much of theoretical theology but little of practical theology—they actually put their theology into practice. This is why the cornerstone of Puritan thought and activity is often thought to be their preaching, which was doctrinally sound and doxologically rich. They were *experiential* in the pulpit, which is to say they combined doctrine and doxology to preach a fuller vision of the Christian life. While demanding that believers fix their eyes on Jesus, the author and finisher of our faith, they called for Christians to live all of their lives unto Christ. This they were able to do because they had been given *all* of Christ for life.

Strong pulpits created strong local bodies, and strong local bodies created strong Christian homes. These were Christians who did more than merely *react* to what was happening around them. They were actively involved and engaged in serving Christ and one another. Their goal was nothing less than the building of biblical communities and establishment of Christian culture. If Jesus would have returned then, despite their trials, He would have found them patiently toiling away in the kingdom of God. He would have found them to be about His Father's business. Oh, that the same would be said of us today!

Learning from Them to Become like Them
You and I can benefit from their example because, like them, we can learn to trust the promises of God more than we trust what our eyes see. They lived by faith rather than by sight (2 Cor. 5:7), and we can learn from them to do the same. They lived by every word that

proceeds forth from the mouth of God rather than subsiding on a steady diet of melodramatic and sensational news stories and gossip. By the grace of God, we as their pupils can learn from their examples to live the same way. As it turns out, hope can effectively be *taught*.

The Puritans' unwavering trust in the Scriptures solidified their faith. Despite the great opposition that stood against them, they believed the conquest of Christ over the earth would be successful primarily because God had promised it would be. When the Lord declared, through the prophet Habakkuk, that "the earth shall be filled with the knowledge of the glory of the LORD, as the waters cover the sea" (Hab. 2:14), they understood that this was a promise to be believed and received, despite what current circumstances said. In fact, current circumstances still have no bearing on the fulfillment of God's Word. We must learn, as the Puritans did, that we serve a God who has decreed the end from the beginning (Isa. 46:10).

Thus, the Puritans were of good and hearty cheer toward the business of evangelism and missions. They believed the Lord Jesus when He had said, "The harvest truly is plenteous, but the labourers are few; pray ye therefore the Lord of the harvest, that he will send forth labourers into his harvest" (Matt. 9:37–38). They didn't view the world as something that was constantly going from bad to worse, but, like John Calvin before them, they viewed it as the theater of God's glory. They saw the earth not as a place to escape from but as a battlefield to advance upon with the sword of God's Word.

As they waited for the fulfillment of all God's promises, they held to a triumphant hope. The Bible was the bedrock of their faith and the rock from which flowed refreshing streams of water and the sweetest of honey for their spiritual nourishment (Ps. 78:20; 81:16; 105:41). We can hold to a triumphant hope because we possess the same Bible they did. We have access to those same streams of living water. We can delight in the same honey from the rock they did, for, as Paul wrote, "All our fathers…did all eat the same spiritual meat; and did all drink the same spiritual drink: for they drank of that spiritual Rock that followed them: and that Rock was Christ" (1 Cor. 10:1, 3–4). In short, we possess the same Christ the Puritans had.

The Triumphant Testimony of Scripture

Scripture does not mince words: Christians will suffer trials. James 1:2-4 says, "My brethren, count it all joy when ye fall into divers temptations; knowing this, that the trying of your faith worketh patience. But let patience have her perfect work, that ye may be perfect and entire, wanting nothing." As much as we do *not* want to face trials, God will often send them for our own good. As our faith is tried and we are taught to patiently wait and hope, our sanctification is happening. God is making us holy.

Likewise, Peter writes, "Beloved, think it not strange concerning the fiery trial which is to try you, as though some strange thing happened unto you: but rejoice, inasmuch as ye are partakers of Christ's sufferings; that, when his glory shall be revealed, ye may be glad also with exceeding joy" (1 Peter 4:12-13). Trials are not to be viewed as some strange thing in the life of the Christian; they are a normal part of being a Christ follower. In fact, according to Peter, trials are cause for rejoicing because they are evidence that we participate in the sufferings of Christ. And, if we participate in His sufferings, will we not also participate in His triumph? "Thanks be to God, which giveth us the victory through our Lord Jesus Christ" (1 Cor. 15:57).

The story line of Scripture seems to fit the paradigm of "wait and hope" quite well. Consider the promise of a coming Messiah, for which the Old Testament saints endured thousands of years of waiting and hoping. They waited for Jesus to come, hoping He would soon fulfill the roles of perfect Prophet, Priest, and King. The New Testament writers wrote with an eager expectation that the gospel would spread, the nations would be discipled, the church would be built, and every last enemy would be conquered and placed beneath the feet of Jesus. Then they wrote of how, at the culmination of these things, Jesus would return in triumphant victory. As we already stated, their waiting and hoping strengthened their resolve all the more to live all of life for Christ, knowing they had been given all of Christ for life.

Today, we continue to wait and hope in the space between Jesus's ascension and return in glory. Like the psalmist, our hearts cry out and sing, "I wait for the LORD, my soul doth wait, and in his word do I hope. My soul waiteth for the Lord more than they that watch for the morning: I say, more than they that watch for the morning. Let Israel hope in the LORD: for with the LORD there is mercy, and with him is plenteous redemption" (Ps. 130:5–7).

The Joy of the Lord Is Our Strength
There is much more that could be written and much more that we will read about the Puritans in the following chapters. But for right now, let it suffice for us to note what made the Puritans tick.

Over the years, my study of the Puritans has led me to conclude that the main reason they possessed such great joy was because they believed and followed Nehemiah 8:10. In this text, the people of Israel are mournful because, after having returned from Babylonian exile, having just rebuilt the wall around Jerusalem, and hearing God's Word read and preached, they realize the depths of their sin and the reason God had judged their nation. But in verse 10, Nehemiah and the other leaders come to the people and say, "Go your way, eat the fat, and drink the sweet, and send portions unto them for whom nothing is prepared: for this day is holy unto our LORD: neither be ye sorry; for the joy of the LORD is your strength." The joy of the Lord was their strength, so they were to feast together and celebrate all the more. Did they deny their troubles? Of course not! But they did redirect their gaze where it belonged: on God and the joy that comes through knowing Him and being known by Him.

This joy of the Lord strengthened and led the Jews of Nehemiah's day into an interval of feasting and drinking together. Puritanism, despite the common misconceptions, exemplifies the joy experienced when Christians fellowship together. Even today, there is something sacred and supremely encouraging that happens when Christians, strengthened by the joy of the Lord, gather together for fellowship around the table to break bread.

The Puritans often did this exact thing. When they were threatened with persecution, famine, incarceration, and death, what did they do? They communally turned to the Lord for renewal, strength, conscience was bound to Scripture consider the possibility of going against it? My experiences in early 2020 taught me the truth that Luther likely wrestled with the night before his trial: the temptation to take the easy way out is forever a real one to battle against.

Having resigned from my position, I suddenly found myself with no source of income to provide for my wife and infant son. I began to search for a job and a church that was doctrinally sound, but as it turned out, both were exceptionally hard to come by. Would moving be necessary?

At the same time, this was early 2020. Rumors of a new respiratory illness were beginning to run rampant, but China is a long way from rural Pennsylvania. I was certain that by spring all that stuff would blow over, I'd be at a church, and our family would be provided for.

Less than a month after my resignation, my wife's grandmother passed away. It had been some time coming, but as is often the case, we were caught somewhat unprepared. I had gone to the hospital to visit her when others could not and held her hand for a short time to comfort her in her confusion. Her passing was not a huge shock, but it was a surprise. We held her funeral on a Friday.

By the middle of the next week, my grandmother—my father's mother—had suddenly passed away too. This was more shocking. We had no idea she was as sick as she was, and her death was unexpected. She went into the hospital one day for what we thought was a routine visit, and she never came out.

Right around that same time, COVID hit full force. In just a few days, everything changed. The world shut down. I started getting emails and phone calls that all the churches I was scheduled to preach at were canceling their services. Search committees began emailing to explain the process was going to be a lengthy one as they prepared to stop holding services. The job market dried up overnight as businesses closed or transitioned to working remotely.

My head was reeling. Forget about what we would do for money—what would we do for fellowship? How would I preach God's Word if every church shut down? What were we to do? Anxiety began to build, but the trials weren't over.

Shortly after the shutdown of 2020, my father found himself in the hospital. Hardly any time at all had passed between my resignation from the church and the passing of two grandparents. Once more, we had no idea what was going on; he'd lost his voice and was having some serious trouble breathing. We knew so little of the new coronavirus that everyone was talking about. We began to wonder: Had he somehow contracted this strange COVID illness?

As the Lord saw fit, no. It was not COVID. He was instead diagnosed with metastasized stage 4 lung cancer and given weeks to live.

From my vantage point, it looked like the world was collapsing. Close family members were dying. I was exhausting finances to make ends meet. Churches were shutting down and I had no say in it. We didn't even have time to join a church before all this happened.

Yet the trials still weren't over. One morning, only a few weeks after my father's diagnosis, my mother woke up and realized her hearing was gone in one ear. Multiple tests followed and doctors discovered a brain tumor.

One day, while I was feeling quite low, I opened up Richard Sibbes's *The Bruised Reed*. I cannot recall one particular part that really stood out, but I do remember how reading it was like balm to my weary and troubled soul. After reading from Sibbes, I opened up Thomas Watson's *Heaven Taken by Storm* and was greatly encouraged by Watson's passion for holiness.

Soon I was reading work after work from the Puritans—some old, some new, all richly rewarding. They reminded me what I had been in danger of forgetting: our hope for triumph is genuine because Christ Himself has triumphed on our behalf.

A few years later, I can testify that the grace of God has been sufficient through every single trial. Churches did not stay closed long, and we were able to fellowship again. In fact, thankfully, one church in our area quickly resumed public worship and invited me to get involved. Doctors determined that my mother's tumor was slow growing and that surgery could be postponed. Treatments for my father started immediately and—praise the Lord—the few weeks that doctors gave him turned into three and a half years. He passed into glory on October 4, 2023, about two weeks after my grandfather, Eugene Tanner, also passed. I had the inestimable privilege of preaching both my grandfather's funeral sermon with my dad present and then, from the same pulpit, preaching my dad's funeral sermon a little over one week later.

I write all this not for pity but to show the reader that suffering, to various degrees, is common to the Christian experience. I have gone through, am going through, and will go through trials, just like you. But in the midst of all these trials, fears, losses, and worries, we can learn the Puritan hope of triumph. Their writings can teach us, just as they've continued to teach me.

Of course, the Puritans are no substitute for the Bible. The Word of God must be our constant companion. For every Sibbes, Watson, and Bunyan, we must find solace in a psalm, an epistle, and a gospel. Indeed, the Psalms teach us to pray with earnest hope. The Gospels offer us true joy as we are reminded of the glory of Christ. The Epistles anchor us in solid truth and doctrine. The Puritans are akin to seasonings, like salt or pepper, that serve to accompany and accentuate these main dishes.

Yes, our constant source of contentment is to be found in Christ alone. As Paul wrote in Philippians 3:7, "But what things were gain to me, those I counted loss for Christ." Christ is the supreme treasure of our souls; we can be truly and eternally content in Him. As we set our eyes on Christ, the Puritans can remind us of the hope we have in Jesus and, on occasion, help us to mine new riches from the caverns of Scripture and reveal glorious treasures we have not yet set eyes on ourselves.

Where This Journey Is Heading
I don't believe the Puritans were better Christians, or holier, or more righteous than any other group of Christians throughout the history of Christendom. I do not pretend that they were the only Christians to suffer persecution or the only ones to cling to hope despite trials, sorrows, and troubles. But I do believe that they have a very peculiar

and uncanny ability to lift the hearts of those sinking in the deep, miry clay through their recorded sermons and writings.

Threatened by the Church of England, the Church of Rome, and the worldly environment that encompassed them, the Puritans knew well the fierce storms that may, at times, assail Christians. They knew the threat of imprisonment for preaching the gospel and the threat of death for following Christ. They were ejected from their churches, caught up in political and religious wars, and displaced from their lands. In short, they knew the dejection of being hated by the world. Despite all this, their fervent hope in the Lord Jesus Christ carried them through every storm with a jovial heart and comforted soul.

Through their experiential and experimental preaching (preaching to both the heart and soul), commitment to the sovereignty of God, and unwavering commitment to Calvinism (the five *solas* and the doctrines of grace), their preaching and writing survives as the historical testimony and record of their faithfulness to Christ, His Word, and His church.

Ultimately, this book is going to examine the lives and writings of various Puritans. We will look to men like Owen, Sibbes, Brooks, Goodwin, Watson, Bunyan, and Edwards. The goal is not that we would worship the men or their times but that they would serve as magnifying glasses that enlarge and make more glorious before our eyes the supreme treasure that is ours in Christ.

On occasion, we will also look to men who do not fit the historical period of the Puritans but who I believe have been blessed with what I refer to as a Puritan-esque spirit. These men may not fit the exact historical or demographical requirements to be called Puritans, but they share in that same powerful spirit and commitment to the Lord Jesus Christ, His sovereign reign and rule over the cosmos, and the Scriptures as the only infallible rule and order for life. They were staunchly committed to the five *solas* of the Reformation (faith alone, grace alone, Scripture alone, Christ alone, and glory to God alone) and the doctrines of grace (total depravity, unconditional election, limited atonement, irresistible grace, and perseverance of the saints).

As we consider how one ought to wait, hope, and serve God in the midst of trial, suffering, and conflict, let us keep at the forefront of our minds the victory that Christ wrought at the cross and the glorious resurrection we are promised to experience one day. This is, after all, the Puritan hope of triumph in the midst of suffering.

Study Questions

1. Read again the quote from Alexandre Dumas's *The Count of Monte Cristo*. Do you have any instances in your own life that have proved the value of waiting on the Lord and hoping in Him for triumph?

2. The Puritans are remembered fondly today for their *experiential* theology, wherein they applied the truths and doctrines of Scripture in very personal and practical ways. What are some immediate steps you can take to begin practicing theology experientially in your own life?

3. Did the Puritans believe Christians are called to an idle life or a militant life? Explain your answer.

4. Read 2 Corinthians 5:7. What does it mean to live by faith rather than sight? How might this impact us as we wait and hope?

5. Our hope, like the Puritans, is in Christ and His triumphant victory. Why does it matter what we hope in?

Chapter 1

The Trial and Triumph of Mortifying the Flesh

Sin can overwhelm a soul. Iniquity, like a flattening iron, can take the most jovial of saints and flatten and crush them until they are mourning in dust and ash.

The glorious truth, however, is this: while sin *should* grieve the Christian, it need not crush the saint. In Jesus, we have a Savior who, once and for all, offered Himself up as a sacrifice for our sins (Heb. 10:12–14). Those who repent of their sin and believe in Jesus, trusting in His atoning death, burial, and resurrection, are truly saved (Mark 1:15; Rom. 10:9). This salvation is based solely on the meritorious and finished work of the Lord Jesus. The sinner does not need to offer works of their own to be saved but must simply have faith in Christ.

Of course, Peter tells us that it is better to suffer for doing well rather than doing evil (1 Peter 3:17). But when we do suffer for sin, it is the chastisement of our heavenly Father upon us. While it is certainly not good to grieve the Holy Spirit by sinning, that grief is evidence of salvation. Grief, however, mustn't stand alone. It ought to lead to godly sorrow and repentance. Psalm 51 is a beautiful example of prayer from a heart both contrite and broken over sin. But we cannot forget that the trials of sin can be triumphed over through faith alone.

Justification by Faith Alone

Before we discuss the trial of overcoming sin, we must make certain we have grasped justification by faith alone. This is one doctrine that the Puritans understood and explained particularly well. William Perkins explained justification this way:

> Justification has two parts: remission of sins and imputation of Christ's righteousness.
>
> Remission of sins is that part of justification whereby he that believes is freed from the guilt and punishment of sin by the passion of Christ....
>
> Imputation of righteousness is the other part of justification, whereby such as believe, having the guilt of their sins covered, are accounted just in the sight of God through Christ's righteousness....
>
> The form of justification is as it were a kind of translation of the believer's sins to Christ and again Christ's righteousness to the believer by a reciprocal or mutual imputation.[1]

Perkins helps us to rightly conclude that our salvation is the result of Christ's finished work and not the result of any work on our behalf. When we are freely justified by God, our sins are borne away by Jesus, who has also exhausted the wrath of God against us. Simultaneously, Jesus's perfect standing before God is imputed to us so that we are declared, legally and actually, righteous in the sight of God. Thus, the apostle Paul wrote that "there is therefore now no condemnation to them which are in Christ Jesus, who walk not after the flesh, but after the Spirit" (Rom. 8:1).

Justification is by faith alone, apart from works (Gal. 2:16). This is, as Martin Luther said, the doctrine on which the church stands or falls. It is also the doctrine that the Christian is perhaps most dependent on. Apart from justification by faith alone, there would be no hope of salvation. This is abundantly good news for the child of God and an incredibly compelling reason for the sinner to repent of their sin and turn quickly to Christ. But let's not pretend that the double imputation of Christ totally eradicates our sin nature when we're saved. It doesn't. As any saint who has been in the trenches for some time can attest, the battle with sin is an ongoing one. So, why do we fight for this battle? Why wrestle temptation and sin if we're

---

1. William Perkins, *A Golden Chain*, in *The Works of William Perkins*, ed. Joel R. Beeke and Greg A. Salazar (Grand Rapids: Reformation Heritage Books, 2018), 6:182.

justified by Christ and all our sins—past, present, and future—are paid in full by Jesus?

Pursuing Holiness
The pursuit of holiness is not about earning salvation; rather, it is the heart cry of the one who has been freely justified by Christ. Faith itself is aroused in the heart by Christ (Rom. 10:17; Gal. 2:20) so that the one who believes in Jesus cannot boast in their ability to believe but must boast in Christ alone, who is the author and finisher of our faith (Heb. 12:1–2). All of this serves as a precious reminder that, in Christ, "though your sins be as scarlet, they shall be as white as snow; though they be red like crimson, they shall be as wool" (Isa. 1:18).

There is, as it were, a transaction that happens between the sinner and Christ when, by faith, the sinner repents of sin and flees to Him as Lord and Savior. As the apostle Paul wrote in 2 Corinthians 5:21, "For he hath made him to be sin for us, who knew no sin; that we might be made the righteousness of God in him." In theology, we refer to this transaction as double imputation: our sins are imputed to Christ and He bears them away, and His righteousness is imputed to us. Yet this is only the initial exchange that takes place at the transaction. There is a lifelong transformation that begins at this point of the exchange as well. In theology, we refer to this lifelong transformation as *sanctification*: the process whereby God continually works through the Holy Spirit to make the saint holy as He is holy. John Calvin understood this transaction and its repercussions well. In his *Institutes* he wrote,

> Why, then, are we justified by faith? Because by faith we grasp Christ's righteousness, by which alone we are reconciled to God. Yet you could not grasp this without at the same time grasping sanctification also. For he "is given unto us for righteousness, wisdom, sanctification, and redemption" [1 Cor. 1:30]. Therefore Christ justifies no one whom he does not at the same time sanctify. These benefits are joined together by an everlasting and indissoluble bond, so that those whom he illumines by his

wisdom, he redeems; those whom he redeems, he justifies; those whom he justifies, he sanctifies.[2]

The sinner justified will be sanctified. That much is certain. The process, however, is often quite arduous. It is filled with trials, sorrows, and hardships. And the more one grows in holiness, the more wretched their sin will appear and the more they will despise the wickedness still present in them.

The question is this: Is there truly a victorious and triumphant hope for the saint battling sin?

Grieved by Sin

If you're at all familiar with the life of John Bunyan, then you know that before he was saved (and perhaps even after, for a time), he wrestled with the grief of his sin. It seemed to him to be an inescapable burden, and the more he thought of it, the more terrified he became. He was plagued by nightmares and a constant fear of death. After all, do the Scriptures not declare that "It is a fearful thing to fall into the hands of the living God" (Heb. 10:31)? The one who has been even partially awakened to their vast iniquity does well to tremble before the holiness of God. To paraphrase R. C. Sproul, even the sin we think the smallest, tiniest, most trivial, and most insignificant is still cosmic treason against the holy God of the cosmos.

Some of the Puritans had an uncanny ability to vividly describe and illustrate just how offensive sin is to God and how terrible the wrath of God truly is against sinners. Jonathan Edwards preached a remarkably well-known sermon about the sinner and God's wrath titled "Sinners in the Hands of an Angry God." This sermon has, by the providential purposes of God, been taught even in secular schools and campus settings as an example of great American rhetoric and writing. But the actual sermon itself is well worth reading for its spiritual, doctrinal, and biblical content, for in it, Edwards expounds on the wrath of God in an extremely lucid way:

---

2. John Calvin, *Institutes of the Christian Religion*, trans. Ford Lewis Battles (Louisville, Ky.: Westminster John Knox Press, 1960), 798 (3.16.1).

God has laid himself under no obligation, by any promise to keep any natural man out of hell one moment. God certainly has made no promises either of eternal life, or of any deliverance or preservation from eternal death, but what are contained in the covenant of grace, the promises that are given in Christ, in whom all the promises are yea and amen. But surely they have no interest in the promises of the covenant of grace who are not the children of the covenant, who do not believe in any of the promises, and have no interest in the Mediator of the covenant.

So that, whatever some have imagined and pretended about promises made to natural men's earnest seeking and knocking, it is plain and manifest, that whatever pains a natural man takes in religion, whatever prayers he makes, till he believes in Christ, God is under no manner of obligation to keep him a moment from eternal destruction.

So that, thus it is that natural men are held in the hand of God, over the pit of hell; they have deserved the fiery pit, and are already sentenced to it; and God is dreadfully provoked, his anger is as great towards them as to those that are actually suffering the executions of the fierceness of his wrath in hell, and they have done nothing in the least to appease or abate that anger, neither is God in the least bound by any promise to hold them up one moment; the devil is waiting for them, hell is gaping for them, the flames gather and flash about them, and would fain lay hold on them, and swallow them up; the fire pent up in their own hearts is struggling to break out: and they have no interest in any Mediator, there are no means within reach that can be any security to them. In short, they have no refuge, nothing to take hold of; all that preserves them every moment is the mere arbitrary will, and uncovenanted, unobliged forbearance of an incensed God.[3]

And there's the compelling reason why we should hate sin. Even after we're saved, justified, and have the righteousness of Christ imputed to us, sin becomes no less offensive to God. Sure, believers are never again in danger of hellfire or God's eternally abounding

---

3. Jonathan Edwards, "Sinners in the Hands of an Angry God," in *The Works of Jonathan Edwards* (Edinburgh: Banner of Truth, 1979), 2:9.

wrath, but why would we want to make a mockery of such a great salvation as this?

Martin Luther, like Bunyan and Edwards, also knew the grief of sin. After he became a monk, and before the Reformation began in full swing, Luther would spend countless hours in his monastery every day confessing his sins to another priest. Now, you might ask the question, "What could a priest possibly do inside of a monastery that would warrant hours of confession?" Evidently, the priest hearing Luther's confessions daily thought the same thing, because he eventually told the young Luther to go away and not come back until he committed a sin large enough worth confessing!

Luther's problem was like Bunyan's. Both men clearly saw their wretchedness and God's holiness but thought that, somehow, they could become righteous on their own. They thought that enough repenting and good works would earn them a right standing before God.

Maybe you can relate. I certainly can.

The Crushing Weight of Sin
I remember a time in my life when, as a teenager steeped in a hybrid theology of Roman Catholicism and Holiness Pentecostal beliefs, my sin seemed destined to keep me separated from Christ. In my poor theological understanding, I thought my lies too many for the truthful Christ to forgive, my anger too much for the meek Jesus to wash away, and my wretched thoughts too ugly for the perfect and beautiful Savior to bear. In short, I thought my sins too many and too great for Christ to be willing to forgive without some effort on my behalf.

You want to know how much grief sin can cause? I honestly believed salvation was something that had to be earned. I thought salvation could be more easily lost than acquired and that unless I repented of every sin I committed, I was a goner. Praise the Lord that, ultimately, these things could not be further from the truth! But my church background had instilled these fearful thoughts in me over the period of a few years.

At one time I had known I was saved by grace alone, but at age fourteen, I was a nervous and trembling wreck before the Lord.

Whenever peace and assurance would come, I'd quickly remind myself of my battle with sin and the things I'd heard in church the last Sunday—things like, "If you sin while driving and get in a wreck and die without repenting, you're going to hell!"—and would lose all peace and assurance I had only moments before. I was like Martin Luther in the confessional. It didn't matter if the sin was seemingly small, or even if no apparent law of God had been broken, I had to confess every apparent sin I could before God to reearn salvation, which—in my mind—I had obviously lost multiple times over throughout the day. Thus, my evenings were filled with prayers of repentance and cries for God's mercies.

One Sunday, I heard a sermon from a visiting pastor who stated that he had reached a state of sinless perfection. He said he hadn't repented in weeks because he hadn't sinned in weeks. This was too much for fourteen-year-old me to bear—I had been bored since entering the church service and was certain I was the most pitiful of sinners. And then there was this preacher in front of me who had attained perfection! Could I, miserable wretch I was, ever find such holiness for myself?

That evening, after spending a few hours on my knees, painstakingly repenting of every sin I could think of, combing over my past for forgotten sins like a dog groomer carefully searching for fleas, I decided it was time to learn the secret of holiness. If that preacher had found the key to never sin again, I wanted it too. But he was gone and there was no one else to ask. It was late. I'd read the Bible through, and 1 John was of immense comfort, but I had been told by former pastors that any sin was enough to remove me from God's good grace. I needed help from someone who could explain the Bible to me.

It literally took years for me to finally understand this, but Luther was the instrumental saint that God used in my life to explain exactly how my sins could be pardoned and I could be justified by God's grace freely. I had already, to some extent, embraced the theology of the Puritans and the Reformers. But, for whatever reason, there was a missing piece for me, and my sins continued to plague me with guilt.

Then, one day, I was sitting in a work cubicle, listening to a biography on Luther, when, in Luther's own words, I heard this:

> I had been possessed by an unusually ardent desire to understand Paul in his epistle to the Romans. Nevertheless, in spite of the ardour of my heart, I was hindered by the unique word in the first chapter: "The righteousness of God...." I hated that word "righteousness of God," because in accordance with the usage and custom of the doctors I had been taught to understand it philosophically as meaning, as they put it, the formal or active righteousness according to which God is righteous and punishes sinners and the unjust.
>
> As a monk I led an irreproachable life. Nevertheless I felt that I was a sinner before God.... Not only did I not love, but I actually hated the righteous God who punishes sinners....
>
> Day and night I tried to meditate upon the significance of these words: "The righteousness of God is revealed in it, as it is written: The righteous shall live by faith." Then, finally, God had mercy on me, and I began to understand that the righteousness of God is that gift of God by which a righteous man lives, namely, faith, and that this sentence—"The righteousness of God is revealed in the Gospel"—is passive, indicating that the merciful God justifies us by faith, as it is written: "The righteous shall live by faith." Now I felt as though I had been reborn altogether and had entered Paradise....
>
> Just as intensely as I had before hated the expression "the righteousness of God," I now lovingly praised this most pleasant word. This passage from Paul became for me the very gate to Paradise.[4]

I had, for years now, struggled to know whether my sins were truly forgiven. But sitting in my gray, plain cubicle, the world seemed to be aglow with beauty as I heard these words. Plain gray walls never looked so good! A warmness rushed over me and, finally, I knew the truth: The just shall live by faith! We are declared righteous by faith!

---

4. Paul R. Spickard and Kevin M. Cragg, *A Global History of Christians* (Grand Rapids: Baker Academic, 1994), 174–75.

It was as though Luther himself had grabbed my hand and taken me through the gates of Paradise with him.

Child of God, if you are in the fiery trial of some temptation or sin, you must fight the battle, but also look to Christ, who is the source of our triumph. This same peace can be yours in Christ.

I recall sometime later, after encountering Luther's words, I came across Bunyan's autobiography, *Grace Abounding to the Chief of Sinners*. He knew what it was to face a great trial of temptation and sin, and he had learned the secret peace that comes to the saint through a knowledge of Christ:

> But one day, as I was passing in the field, and that too with some dashes on my conscience, fearing lest yet all was not right, suddenly this sentence fell upon my soul, Thy righteousness is in heaven; and methought withal, I saw with the eyes of my soul, Jesus Christ at God's right hand: there, I say, was my righteousness; so that wherever I was, or whatever I was doing, God could not say of me, He wants My righteousness; for that was just before Him. I also saw moreover, that it was not my good frame of heart that made my righteousness better, nor yet my bad frame that made my righteousness worse; for my righteousness was Jesus Christ Himself, The same yesterday, to-day, and for ever. Heb. xiii. 8.
>
> Now did my chains fall off my legs indeed; I was loosed from my afflictions and irons; my temptations also fled away; so that from that time those dreadful scriptures of God left off to trouble me: now went I also home rejoicing, for the grace and love of God; so when I came home, I looked to see if I could find that sentence; Thy righteousness is in heaven, but could not find such a saying; wherefore my heart began to sink again, only that was brought to my remembrance, 1 Cor. i. 30, Christ Jesus, who of God is made unto us wisdom, and righteousness, and sanctification, and redemption; by this word I saw the other sentence true.[5]

---

5. John Bunyan, *Grace Abounding to the Chief of Sinners*, in *The Works of John Bunyan* (Edinburgh: Banner of Truth, 1991), 1:35–36.

When we are grieved by the trials of temptation and sin, we must look to Christ! As we wait and hope for the total triumph still to come, it is to Christ we must turn. Because Bunyan knew the grace of God in an extraordinary way, he was able to pen these encouraging words of Christ's power to save: "Sinner, thou thinkest that because of thy sins and infirmities I cannot save thy soul, but behold My Son is by Me, and upon Him I look and not on thee, and will deal with thee according as I am pleased with Him."[6]

Triumphing over Sin

If you know Christ as your Lord and Savior, your sins are indeed paid for. But the sin nature still exists. Though we must be comforted by our salvation found freely in Christ, we must not grow complacent with sin. While we must turn to Christ as our hope and strength, there is diligent effort that must be exercised on our behalf (Phil. 2:12–13).

Thomas Brooks offers a simple tactic to war against sin and triumph over it in his *Precious Remedies against Satan's Devices*:

> Remedy (1). First, Keep at the greatest distance from sin, and from playing with the golden bait which Satan holds forth to catch you; for this you have (Romans xii. 9), "Abhor that which is evil, cleave to that which is good." When we meet with anything extremely evil and contrary to us, nature abhors it, and retires as far as it can from it. The Greek word that is there rendered "abhor," is very significant; it signifies to hate it as hell itself, to hate it with horror....
>
> The best course to prevent falling into the pit is to keep at the greatest distance from it; he who will be so bold as to attempt to dance upon the brink of the pit, may find by woeful experience that it is a righteous thing with God that he should fall into the pit. Joseph keeps at a distance from sin, and from playing with Satan's golden baits, and stands. David draws near, and plays with the bait, and falls, and swallows bait and hook! David comes near the snare, and is taken in it, to the breaking of his

---

6. Bunyan, *Grace Abounding*, 1:258.

bones, the wounding of his conscience, and the loss of fellowship with his God.

Sin is a plague, yes, the worst and most infectious plague in the world; and yet, ah! how few are there who tremble at it—who keep at a distance from it! (1 Cor. v. 6)—"Know ye not that a little leaven leaveneth the whole lump?" As soon as one sin had seized upon Adam's heart, all sin entered into his soul and infested it. How has Adam's one sin spread over all mankind! (Romans v. 12)—"Wherefore by one man sin entered into the world, and death by sin, and so death passed upon all men, for that all have sinned." Ah, how doth the father's sin infect the child, the husband's infect the wife, the master's the servant! The sin that is in one man's heart is able to infect a whole world, it is of such a spreading and infectious nature.[7]

We are under grace and not under the law, yet sin must be killed. It is an infectious disease. It must be avoided. It would kill the world if it could. It must be abhorred. There is nothing more miserable than sin.

Sin cannot be permitted to run rampant. We must flee from it (2 Tim. 2:22). Likewise, when we "resist the devil...he will flee from you" (James 4:7).

Battle lines must be drawn and a war fought. Though the trial be arduous, we must continue to fight the temptations all the same, knowing triumph is ours. The apostle Paul spoke of the need to fight sin in Romans 6:1–4:

> What shall we say then? Shall we continue in sin, that grace may abound? God forbid. How shall we, that are dead to sin, live any longer therein? Know ye not, that so many of us as were baptized into Jesus Christ were baptized into his death? Therefore we are buried with him by baptism into death: that like as Christ was raised up from the dead by the glory of the Father, even so we also should walk in newness of life.

---

7. Thomas Brooks, *Precious Remedies against Satan's Devices*, in *The Works of Thomas Brooks*, ed. Alexander B. Grossart (Edinburgh: James Nichol, 1861–1867), 1:13–14.

We Must Beat *Sin (Rom. 6:1–2)*

"What shall we say then?" is a rhetorical question. We already know the answer: God forbid we continue to sin that grace may abound!

No language could be stronger than this. God, absolutely forbid it; God, do not let it happen; God, it must not be so. Why such strong language? God demands nothing short of perfect holiness. It is a demand that, frankly, we cannot meet. Cue some of Jesus's most challenging statements and the shocked responses of sinners:

> "You must be born again."
>
> "But Jesus, how is this possible?"
>
> "It would be easier for a camel to enter the eye of a needle than for a rich man to enter heaven."
>
> "But Jesus, who then shall be saved?"

In part, the point is that God's standard for holiness is so significant, so great, so perfect that we cannot meet the standard. Thus, we need a Savior who can do what we could never hope to do. Whereas we cannot even go a day, or a few moments, without sinning, we need a Savior who never has and never will sin.

Christ is this Savior. And how does He purchase our salvation? On a bloody cross.

Christ died for our sin so that we might live for Him. To continue now in sin, as though Christ did not die for us, and as though we have not died to sin, is a terribly sinful thing to do. But those who are truly saved should recognize a deeper truth. Because Christ loves us and we now love Him, we should have new desires; specifically, we should desire to be holy!

John Owen wrote of the joy that Christ has in His holy saints in *Communion with God*: "Now, Christ delights exceedingly in his saints: 'As the bridegroom rejoiceth over the bride, so shall thy God rejoice over thee' (Isa. lxii:5).… His heart is glad in us without sorrow. And every day whilst we live is his wedding day…thoughts of communion with the saints were the joy of his heart from eternity."[8]

---

8. John Owen, *Communion with God*, in *The Works of John Owen* (Edinburgh: Banner of Truth, 1965), 2:118.

What an immense joy it is to know that Christ delights in us! This joy is only increased when we walk in holiness. Because we ought to delight in what Christ delights in, we must strive to be holy. We must fight sin. Let us wage war against it. Like Jesus violently chasing money changers from the temple to purge and cleanse it with a whip, let us do violence to the sin in our lives.

Christians must "mortify therefore [our] members which are upon the earth" (Col. 3:5). As Owen famously wrote, "Do you mortify; do you make it your daily work; be always at it whilst you live; cease not a day from this work; be killing sin or it will be killing you."[9] We must be about this business because of what Paul writes in Romans 6.

We Were Baptized into Christ (Rom. 6:3)

John Owen warns that indwelling sin "is an aversation…unto God and everything of God."[10] But we have been baptized into Christ. Such "aversation" must be destroyed at all costs.

Paul understands our baptism into Christ as a spiritual reality. We were dead in trespasses and sins, but Christ made us alive. How? By making us die to sin, that we might live in Him.

Jesus said in John 12:24, "Verily, verily, I say unto you, Except a corn of wheat fall into the ground and die, it abideth alone: but if it die, it bringeth forth much fruit." Saint, as you war against sin and go through these stubborn trials, your triumph depends on this: you must effectively die to sin spiritually, that you might rise to the new life you have in Christ.

Paul puts it like this in Galatians 2:20: "I am crucified with Christ: nevertheless I live; yet not I, but Christ liveth in me: and the life which I now live in the flesh I live by the faith of the Son of God, who loved me, and gave himself for me." When we were saved, we were

---

9. John Owen, *Of the Mortification of Sin in Believers*, in *The Works of John Owen* (Edinburgh: Banner of Truth, 1965), 6:9.

10. John Owen, *The Nature, Power, Deceit, and Prevalency of the Remainders of Indwelling Sin in Believers*, in *The Works of John Owen* (Edinburgh: Banner of Truth, 1966), 6:182.

crucified with Christ. This is part of what it means to be baptized by the Holy Spirit into Christ.

How does this act of spiritual baptism begin? Since it is simultaneous with our justification, the instrument is the same: We were baptized into Christ by faith. Not by working really hard for it. Not by catapulting ourselves into some life of extreme poverty and piety. No, simple faith alone is what unites the lost sinner to Christ. Consider, as Martin Luther wrote in his famous *Commentary on Galatians*, how we are joined to Christ by faith:

> If thou wilt be saved, thou mayest not seek salvation by works: "for God hath sent his only begotten Son into the world, that we might live through him. He was crucified and died for thee, and offered up thy sins in his own body." Here is no congruence or work done before grace, but wrath, sin, terror and death. Wherefore the law doth nothing else but utter sin, terrify and humble, and by this means prepareth us for justification, and driveth us to Christ. For God hath revealed unto us by his word, that he will be unto us a merciful father, and without our deserts (seeing we can deserve nothing) will freely give unto us remission of sins, righteousness, and life everlasting for Christ his Son's sake. For God giveth his gifts freely unto all men, and that is the praise and glory of his divinity.[11]

This is not only an excellent description of our salvation but a summary of what spiritual baptism entails in Christ. As the waters of salvation wash over us by the work of the Holy Spirit, Christ also brings us spiritual gifts, like forgiveness of sins, righteousness, everlasting life, and union with Him. Our triumph over sin is by faith.

The baptismal union between us and Christ is the basis of our richest, most treasured hopes; namely, that we will one day gaze on the glory of our Savior face-to-face, and sin will be no more.

---

11. Martin Luther, *Commentary on Saint Paul's Epistle to the Galatians*, trans. Rev. Erasmus Middleton (Grand Rapids: Eerdmans, 1930), 108.

We Were Buried with Christ in Death (Rom. 6:4)

We mustn't neglect the fact that Jesus truly died at Calvary. He truly was buried for three days, and by virtue of being joined to Him, we were buried as well. This means He truly did die for us, He truly did rise for us, and we truly do share in His victory.

Because of our burial with Christ, sin no longer holds sway over us. We were born slaves to sin (John 8:34). This slavery to sin led to death. Yet Christ provided a means of freedom from this slavery. As 1 Corinthians 15:22 promises, though we were dead in Adam, we are made alive in Christ.

We who have been set free by Jesus are truly free from sin (John 8:36). Sin no longer holds us captive; Christ does. Ironically, our truest freedom is found in being slaves to Christ and righteousness rather than slaves to sin (Rom. 6:18).

It is as though Jesus went to the slave market of sin with particular names and faces on His mind, and finding us, one by one, He called us by name and paid our debt in full so that we would belong to Him. How could we then return to our former master of sin and serve him once more?

You who would kill sin, think on these truths. As Owen wrote, "By faith fill thy soul with a due consideration of that *provision* which is laid up in Jesus Christ for this end and purpose, that all thy lusts, this very lust wherewith thou art entangled, may be mortified."[12] These are the truths whereby we overcome the trials and sorrows of sin.

We Were Birthed to New Life in Christ (Rom. 6:4)

The trials of sin may be fierce, but the question is, How shall we then live? Paul answers by commanding us to walk in newness of life, for now we walk as those who have died to sin and have been raised in new life in Jesus. Just as the Christian's tomb on earth acts as a womb whereby they will one day burst forth in resurrected glory, so too did our spiritual baptism with Christ act as a womb that brought us forth into new life with Jesus.

---

12. Owen, *Of the Mortification of Sin*, 6:79.

This spiritual reality of baptism in Christ has far-reaching consequences, eternal consequences. For those who have been raised to new life in Christ will never perish. We will live forever in union with our Lord. Therefore, we do not sin in order for grace to abound. Rather, because grace has abounded toward us as sinners, and continues to abound daily so that day by day we live in the power of God's sustaining and persevering grace, we aim to live a life that is pleasing to Christ and a reflection of who we are as Christians. We have died and our old master has no hold over us. We belong to Christ, and thus we live for Christ. We aim to kill sin.

Besides the obvious resistance and sin slaying that must take place, what else is there to do? Well, as those who have been baptized into Christ, we have direct access to Him. This can mean only one thing: The saint who waits and hopes and battles through the many trials of temptation and sin must be a saint of *prayer*. Prayer is to the soul as oxygen is to the body. As Thomas Watson wrote,

> We must offer violence to Satan by PRAYER. We overcome him upon our knees. As Samson called to Heaven for help, so a Christian by prayer fetches in auxiliary forces from Heaven. In all temptations, go to God by prayer. "Lord, teach me to use every piece of the spiritual armor; how to hold the shield, how to wear the helmet, how to use the sword of the Spirit. Lord, strengthen me in the battle; let me rather die a conqueror than be taken prisoner, and led by Satan in triumph!" Thus we must offer violence to Satan. There is "a lion in the way," but we must resolve upon fighting.
>
> And let this encourage us to offer violence to Satan. Our enemy is beaten in part already. Christ, who is "the captain of our salvation," has given Satan his death-wound upon the cross, Col. ii. 15. The serpent is soonest killed in his head. Christ has bruised the head of the old Serpent! He is a chained enemy, and a conquered enemy; therefore do not fear him. "Resist the devil, and he will flee from you!" James iv. 7. "The God of peace will soon crush Satan under your feet!" Romans xvi. 20.[13]

---

13. Thomas Watson, *Heaven Taken by Storm: Showing the Holy Violence a Christian Is to Put Forth in the Pursuit after Glory* (Grand Rapids: Soli Deo Gloria, 1992), 42.

Let us pray to Christ, the great Champion of our souls, who overcame temptation in the wilderness (Matt. 4), who has been tempted in every way we are and is still without sin (Heb. 4:14–16), and the very Savior who will bring about the fullness of His conquest over sin and Satan. Let us, though bruised, bleeding, and beaten, look to Christ for our victory over sin. In Him, our waiting and hoping will turn to the defeat of sin. We will be victorious.

Our desire ought to be to taste this victory over sin—now. We should pray that sin would not hold sway or dominion over us and that, by God's grace, we would learn to daily crucify our flesh in our walk with Christ. Below is a prayer from Matthew Henry that will help us seek the favor of the Lord in these ways:

> O let no iniquity have dominion over us, because we are not under the law, but under grace.
>
> Let the flesh be crucified in us, with its affections and lusts, that walking in the Spirit we may not fulfill the lusts of the flesh.
>
> Let our old man be crucified with Christ, that the body of sin may be destroyed, that henceforth we may not serve sin: and let not sin reign in our mortal bodies (in our immortal souls) that we should obey it in the lusts thereof. But being made free from sin, let us become the servants of righteousness.
>
> Let the law of the Spirit of life, which is in Christ Jesus, make us free from the law of sin and death.
>
> Give us grace to put off the old man which is corrupt according to the deceitful lusts, that we may put on the new man, which after God is created in righteousness and true holiness. That the world may be crucified to us, and we to the world by the cross of Christ.[14]

---

14. Matthew Henry, *A Method for Prayer: Freedom in the Face of God* (Fearn, Scotland: Christian Heritage, 1994), 58.

Study Questions

1. What is the doctrine of justification by faith alone? How does it help us to battle sin?

2. Why is it so important for the Christian to pursue holiness and put sin to death?

3. Why does sin so often appear crushing in its weight?

4. Read 1 Peter 3:17. How should we respond when we suffer for doing good? How should we respond when we suffer for having sinned?

5. Read Psalm 51. Coupled with the quotations from this chapter, how does this psalm speak to the nature of waiting and hoping in God when we are being grieved by sin? What is it that we are waiting and hoping for?

Chapter 2

Fighting for Faith and Assurance When Battling Unbelief

In the previous chapter, as we discussed the various trials that surround our battle with sin and the hope we have in Christ, we alluded to another trial we often face as well: the battle for assurance of salvation.

One of the greatest trials that any Christian faces in this life is the battle for true assurance. The one who grasps hold of assurance has a true treasure. They *know* that they are saved. They *know* that they are Christ's. They can say, "I am my beloved's and my beloved is mine" (Song 6:3). It was of this verse that James Durham wrote,

> Faith is still a refuge; when all God's dispensations, and every thing in the believer's case, seems to leave the heart in disquietness, faith is then the last and great refuge. Faith is then most satisfying when repentance is exercised, and all other means diligently gone about; therefore may she now cast this anchor, after she hath been in the exercise of repentance.... Faith will sustain souls in duty...even when they are out of it; faith preserves from fainting under discouragements in the way of God.[1]

The one who possesses the faith described here, which is a true knowledge of union with God, will be made happy and blessed through even the fiercest storms and trials. But the one who lacks assurance is like a ship that, though it is sturdy and in no danger of capsizing, feels as though it may just crumble at even the tiniest of waves.

---

1. James Durham, *The Song of Solomon*, The Geneva Series of Commentaries (Edinburgh: Banner of Truth, 1982), 337.

The one without assurance of salvation meets even the smallest afflictions and sufferings with trembling and trepidation. They are like the elephant afraid of the mouse, for they know not what strength they possess in Christ.

A Christian needs assurance of salvation. Indeed, a lack of it may just be the worst suffering one can experience. So, where does the Christian begin? Where do we turn to?

My Help Comes Not from the Hills
The Psalms are always pertinent for the Christian life, but they are especially appropriate for the saint who is suffering. Just about every imaginable trial is mentioned within their pages. Death? Check. Sin? Check. Enemies? Check. Gossip? Check. It's all there.

It should be of little surprise that lack of assurance is also within the Psalms. But one of the most helpful psalms when we battle for assurance is Psalm 121:1–2, which begins, "I will lift up mine eyes unto the hills, from whence cometh my help. My help cometh from the LORD, which made heaven and earth." What a wonderful reminder! Our help is from the Lord, not from anything within us or anything on this earth.

Often, when we are waiting and hoping, patiently enduring tribulation, we take our eyes off what truly matters. We turn away from Christ and look instead to ourselves, or we look to our situation, or we look to others around us. The problem is that each of those things will fail and let us down.

If you want assurance, the last thing you want to do is look to yourself. You'll never measure up!

If you want assurance, you definitely do not want to look to others. Their faith, or lack thereof, is their own. It won't take very long to convince yourself that you're either far better or far worse than they are.

If you want assurance, this world will be of no help to you at all. Charles Dickens began his *Tale of Two Cities* with that sentiment, "It was the best of times, it was the worst of times," because we never quite understand what times we're actually living in. We are poor judges of experience. Besides, if we think that our situations or emotions are good indicators to determine whether we have assurance of salvation, then we will be let down, time and again. This world knows nothing of the gospel, and our hearts are easily deceived. As Samuel Rutherford wrote, "Your heart is not the compass Christ saileth by. He will give you leave to sing as you please, but he will not dance to your tune. It is not referred to you and your thoughts, what Christ will do with the charters betwixt you and him. Your own misbelief hath torn them, but he hath the principle in heaven with himself. Your thoughts are no parts of the new covenant; dreams change not Christ."[2]

The immutable Christ depends not on our hearts, thoughts, or feelings to save our souls. We cannot change Him with our dreams or nightmares. He is truly a solid rock, and our assurance must be sought in Him alone. So, as we wait and hope, Psalm 121:1–2 reminds us to set our eyes on Jesus! Our hope comes from Him.

Our Hope Comes from the Lord

Have you ever noticed what the writer of Hebrews does in chapter 12? After creating a certified Faith Hall of Fame in chapter 11, he opens chapter 12 by writing,

> Wherefore seeing we also are compassed about with so great a cloud of witnesses, let us lay aside every weight, and the sin which doth so easily beset us, and let us run with patience the race that is set before us, looking unto Jesus the author and finisher of our faith; who for the joy that was set before him endured the cross, despising the shame, and is set down at the right hand of the throne of God. (vv. 1–2)

In other words, while we may gain encouragement from the saints around us and those who came before, our hope must be firmly centered in Jesus Christ alone. Those saints around us and before us did not save us; Christ did. Their lives and teaching are meant to

---

2. Samuel Rutherford, *Letters of Samuel Rutherford* (repr., Edinburgh: Banner of Truth, 1981), 350.

point us to Christ. The moment we begin to worship them, we have a serious problem.

Thus, we look not to the hills or the mountains or the sky, but we look to Christ alone. He is the author and finisher of our faith. He began the story and He will finish the story (Phil. 1:6). If you want assurance, you must look to Christ and remember what He accomplished at the cross.

Though it is an Old Testament passage, Isaiah 53 perfectly prophesied what Jesus would accomplish. It is worth regularly meditating on these words:

> For he shall grow up before him as a tender plant, and as a root out of a dry ground: he hath no form nor comeliness; and when we shall see him, there is no beauty that we should desire him. He is despised and rejected of men; a man of sorrows, and acquainted with grief: and we hid as it were our faces from him; he was despised, and we esteemed him not. Surely he hath borne our griefs, and carried our sorrows: yet we did esteem him stricken, smitten of God, and afflicted. But he was wounded for our transgressions, he was bruised for our iniquities: the chastisement of our peace was upon him; and with his stripes we are healed. All we like sheep have gone astray; we have turned every one to his own way; and the LORD hath laid on him the iniquity of us all. He was oppressed, and he was afflicted, yet he opened not his mouth: he is brought as a lamb to the slaughter, and as a sheep before her shearers is dumb, so he openeth not his mouth. He was taken from prison and from judgment: and who shall declare his generation? for he was cut off out of the land of the living: for the transgression of my people was he stricken. And he made his grave with the wicked, and with the rich in his death; because he had done no violence, neither was any deceit in his mouth. Yet it pleased the LORD to bruise him; he hath put him to grief: when thou shalt make his soul an offering for sin, he shall see his seed, he shall prolong his days, and the pleasure of the LORD shall prosper in his hand. He shall see of the travail of his soul, and shall be satisfied: by his knowledge shall my righteous servant justify many; for he shall bear their iniquities. (vv. 2–11)

When we read this text, how our anxious souls ought to be comforted, our restless hearts stilled, and our weary consciences soothed! Christ, our great Lord and Savior, purchased our redemption at the cross. He paid for our own iniquity. We are healed in Him, which is to say, our sins are forgiven, and we are made righteous before God. We are granted eternal life in Christ.

All this is possible only because Christ *finished* the work. Consider Jesus's own words on the cross when, in John 19:30, He said, "It is finished: and he bowed his head, and gave up the ghost." Jesus finished the work of our redemption; He didn't just do a part and then say, "Now, you go and do the rest." He didn't do 99 percent and say, "You've got the remaining 1 percent." No, the work is finished. He came to accomplish our salvation, and He did not bow His head and give up the ghost until He had done what He came to do.

This is what we must set our eyes on. Our justification is entirely dependent on Christ and His finished work. As Matthew Henry wrote of John 19:1–18,

> It is good for every one with faith, to behold Christ Jesus in his sufferings. Behold him, and love him; be still looking unto Jesus. Did their hatred sharpen their endeavours against him? and shall not our love for him quicken our endeavours for him and his kingdom? Pilate seems to have thought that Jesus might be some person above the common order. Even natural conscience makes men afraid of being found fighting against God. As our Lord suffered for the sins both of Jews and Gentiles, it was a special part of the counsel of Divine Wisdom, that the Jews should first purpose his death, and the Gentiles carry that purpose into effect. Had not Christ been thus rejected of men, we had been for ever rejected of God. Now was the Son of man delivered into the hands of wicked and unreasonable men. He was led forth for us, that we might escape. He was nailed to the cross, as a Sacrifice bound to the altar. The Scripture was fulfilled; he did not die at the altar among the sacrifices, but among criminals sacrificed to public justice. And now let us pause, and with faith look upon Jesus. Was ever sorrow like unto his sorrow? See him

bleeding, see him dying, see him and love him! love him, and live to him![3]

Love Christ and live to Christ. That is the heart of the Christian life. If you want assurance, this is as good a place as any to begin. Look to Christ, love Christ, and live to Christ.

Strengthening the Eyes

Some people reading this may think, "I wish I could look to Him, I really do. But my eyes of faith are just so weak." Richard Sibbes understood the struggle of weak faith. He knew how often we long for a greater degree of faith. But he saw *weak* faith as no hinderance to assurance. After all, any degree of faith at all is still saving faith. As Sibbes wrote,

> As the strongest faith may be shaken, so the weakest, where truth is, is so far rooted that it will prevail. Weakness with watchfulness will stand, when strength with too much confidence fails. Weakness, with acknowledgement of it, is the fittest seat and subject for God to perfect his strength in; for consciousness of our infirmities drives us out of ourselves to him in whom our strength lies.
>
> From this it follows that weakness may be consistent with the assurance of salvation. The disciples, notwithstanding all their weaknesses, are bidden to rejoice that their names are written in heaven (Luke 10:20). Failings, with conflict, in sanctification should not weaken the peace of our justification and assurance of salvation. It matters not so much what ill is in us, as what good; not what corruptions, but how we regard them; not what our particular failings are so much as what the thread and tenor of our lives are, for Christ's dislike of that which is amiss in us turns not to the hatred of our persons but to the victorious subduing of all our infirmities.

---

3. Matthew Henry, *Matthew Henry's Concise Commentary* (John 19:1–18), Christian Classics Ethereal Library, accessed December 2, 2023, https://ccel.org/ccel/henry/mhcc/mhcc.xxxv.xix.html?highlight=John%2019&queryID=30385509&resultID=133298#highlight.

Some have, after conflict, wondered at the goodness of God that so little and such trembling faith should have upheld them in so great combats, when Satan had almost caught them. And, indeed, it is to be wondered at, how much a little grace will prevail with God for acceptance, and over our enemies for victory, if the heart is upright. Such is the goodness of our sweet Saviour that he delights still to show his strength in our weakness.[4]

Remember, it's not the size of the faith that saves but the worth of the Savior. And, thanks be to God, we have a Savior in Jesus who is infinitely more valuable than we could ever begin to imagine.

Adoption: A Means of Great Comfort and Assurance

As we fight for assurance, we look to Jesus. We see the salvation He has wrought. We understand that it is through this salvation we have been justified by faith. But if there's one doctrine that can truly soothe the affliction of the unassured saint, it is the doctrine of *adoption*. We who have been justified have been adopted into God's family, and we can now cry out, "Abba, Father" (Rom. 8:15; Gal. 4:6). We have such a deep intimacy with the Father that we are in no danger of being forgotten or cast off.

William Perkins, explaining how the doctrines of justification and adoption are interrelated, offers very comforting words of assurance to the saint:

> By means of adoption God has bestowed many notable privileges upon His children. (1) They are the Lord's heir apparent. "If we be children, we be also heirs, even the heirs of God" (Rom. 8:17).
>
> (2) They are fellow heirs with Christ, yea kings. "And made us kings and priests, even to God his Father" (Rev. 1:6).
>
> (3) All their affliction, yea even their wants and offenses are turned to trials or fatherly chastisements, inflicted upon them for their good. "And we know that all things work together for good to them that love God, to them who are the called

---

4. Richard Sibbes, *The Bruised Reed*, rev. ed. (Edinburgh: Banner of Truth, 1998), 96–97.

according to his purpose.[…] As it is written, For thy sake we are killed all the day long; we are accounted as sheep for the slaughter. Nay, in all these things we are more than conquerors through him that loved us" (Rom. 8:28, 36–37)....

(4) They have dominion over all creatures, yet so as that in this life they have only right to the thing, but after this life they shall have right in the same....

Last of all, they have angels as ministering spirits attending upon them for their good.[5]

Our adoption brings us back to Song of Songs 6:3. We can literally cry out, "I am my beloved's, and my beloved is mine." Adoption secures us to Christ. The one who knows this can have assurance. Or, if doubts arise and tears begin to stream down the cheeks, yet we can pray, "Lord, I believe; help thou mine unbelief" (Mark 9:24).

Triumphing in the Battle for Assurance

What can we say to comfort the saint who is battling for assurance? What word of hope can we offer to the saint who, weary from battle, feels they have very little left to give? What manifestation of grace may be poured out on the storm-tossed saint who, fiercely oaring against the stormy waves, has sweat out what they believe to be their last ounce of strength?

John Owen may have written fiercely about the great need to mortify the flesh and kill sin, but he also wrote exhortations of encouragement. We now turn our attention to Owen and his wonderful, albeit lesser known, *Exposition of Psalm CXXX* (Psalm 130). This particular psalm offers wonderful assurance to the saints of God regarding their salvation in Christ, and Owen, knowing the great need for assurance of salvation in the saint, writes lucidly about how one may go about attaining such assurance. But before we turn our attention to these steps to gain assurance, and by way of exhortation, let us first turn our attention to one of his warnings. Expositing verse 4 ("But there is forgiveness with thee, that thou mayest be feared") he writes,

---

5. Perkins, *Golden Chain*, 6:184–85.

Now, unless a man do duly consider the tenor of the covenant wherein we walk with God, and the nature of that gospel obedience which he requires at our hands, with the state and condition which is our lot and portion whilst we live in this world, the daily sense of these, with the trouble that must be undergone on their account, may keep him in the dark unto himself, and hinder him from the establishment in believing which otherwise he might attain unto. On this account, some as holy persons as any in this world, being wholly taken up with the consideration of these homebred perplexities, and not clearly acquainted with the way and tenor of assuring their souls before God according to the rule of the covenant of grace, have passed away their days in a bondage-frame of spirit, and unacquaintance with that strong consolation which God is abundantly willing that all the heirs of promise should receive.[6]

Owen understood the issue rather well. Even those saints who, battered and bloodied, have been fighting off temptation and working to slay sin will often have no sense of assurance because they do not consider the covenant of grace wherein we have been placed. When our attention is fixated only on the temptation, the sin, the stumbling falls, and our lack of perfection, assurance is the last thing we feel. Instead, we feel desperately cold, alone, and defeated. But as we go through the many trials of battling sin, it is not God's will that we should have no consolation or assurance. On the contrary, He desires to abundantly bless us with such knowledge.

Throughout his exposition of Psalm 130, Owen notes a few important things that the Christian can do to find assurance, even while battling temptations and sins. While the whole exposition is worth studying, he offers two "rules" for this particular exercise in coming to a state of assurance.

Owen's first rule is, "Be not judge of your own condition, but let Christ judge."[7] This is, perhaps, the most important matter when it comes to finding assurance. If you judge your own spiritual

---

6. John Owen, *An Exposition upon Psalm CXXX*, in *The Works of John Owen* (Edinburgh: Banner of Truth, 1966), 6:551.
7. Owen, *Exposition upon Psalm CXXX*, 6:542.

condition, and honestly weigh your sin, sense of worth, and value before the Lord, you will always come up short. Praise the Lord, then, that our salvation is not dependent on our good works, lack of sin, or extent of faith. No, our salvation is dependent solely on the object of our faith—namely, Jesus Christ Himself.

The truth of the matter is that we are quite awful judges anyway. We shouldn't want the job. We are the sick patients who, in illness, discover a madness of the mind that makes sound judgments nearly impossible. Left to our own devices, we will continually misdiagnose. What we need is the balm of Gilead to calm our troubled and unsettled souls, and this balm only Christ can prescribe and apply.

We, the sick patients, need a most glorious Physician to rightly discern our disease, prescribe and apply a cure, and make us well. Jesus is this Physician. Thus, Owen could write,

> You are invited to take the comfort of this gospel truth, that "there is forgiveness with God." You say, not for you.... This false judgment, made by souls in their entanglements, of their own condition, is oftentimes a most unconquerable hinderance unto the bettering of it. They fill themselves with thoughts of their own about it, and on them they dwell, instead of looking out after a remedy. Misgiving thoughts of their distempers are commonly a great part of some men's sickness. Many diseases are apt to cloud the thoughts, and to cause misapprehensions concerning their own nature and danger. And these delusions are a real part of the person's sickness. Nature is no less impaired and weakened by them, the efficacy of remedies no less obstructed, than by any other real distemper. In such cases we persuade men to acquiesce in the judgment of their skillful physician; not always to be wasting themselves in and by their own tainted imaginations, and so despond upon their own mistakes, but to rest in what is informed them by him who is acquainted with the causes and tendency of their indisposition better than themselves. It is ofttimes one part of the soul's depths to have false apprehensions of its condition.[8]

---

8. Owen, *Exposition upon Psalm CXXX*, 6:542–43.

Indeed, Owen is right. The sinner will convince himself to be a saint and the saint will convince themselves to still be in throngs of sin, lost and undone. Owen even says that sin is like a madness that causes "some [to] say they are lost for ever, when God is with them."[9] So, take your eyes off the sin, the trial, the discouragement, the distemper, and whatever else is causing your spiritual madness. Instead, set your eyes on Christ, that great and glorious Physician, who will apply the balm and bring a most peaceful and restful assurance where before there was only doubt.

Yet to totally forget oneself is not the mark of a true Christian. To do so would likely lead into all manner of sin as the Christian, ignorant of all around him, would subsequently lead a selfish and sinful lifestyle. This would be a false assurance. So, even as we set our eyes on Christ as the Physician of our souls, knowing we are justified by faith and not by works (Gal. 2:16), it is still good to evaluate our own condition and make certain we are following the Physician's orders and our own condition is improving (e.g., Ex. 20:1–17; Matt. 5–7; 22:34–40).

Here's the problem, though: such examination, almost inevitably, will lead to cruel judgments of ourselves. So, Owen makes it clear in his second rule that "self-condemnation and abhorrence do very well consist with gospel justification and peace."[10] In other words, the one who experiences hatred toward their remaining sin, who is entangled in a battle against temptation, and who is warring against the deeds of the flesh is exhibiting the true characteristics of a Christian and may also come to possess true peace through the justification wrought in their lives by the power of the gospel.

The best thing to do in such matters is to look to Christ and remember His great covenant of redemption, formed between Himself, the Father, and the Spirit. We must remember that, in eternity past, it was the Father who planned our salvation, promising to gift us to the Son at just the right time (John 6:37). Then, when the fullness of time had come, the Father sent the Son into the world to take

---

9. Owen, *Exposition upon Psalm CXXX*.
10. Owen, *Exposition upon Psalm CXXX*, 6:547.

on the form of flesh in order to purchase our redemption and adoption as sons and daughters of God (Gal. 4:4–5). Now, the Holy Spirit procures us unto Christ when, through the preaching of the Word of God, He revives us and draws us to Christ, acting forevermore as the seal and guarantee of our eternal salvation (2 Cor. 1:22; 5:5; Eph. 1:13–14; 4:30). As the Savoy Declaration (a Congregational amendment to the Westminster Confession of Faith) put it,

> It pleased God, in his eternal purpose, to choose and ordain the Lord Jesus, his only-begotten Son, according to a covenant made between them both, to be the Mediator between God and man; the Prophet, Priest, and King; the Head and Saviour of his Church, the Heir of all things, and Judge of the world; unto whom he did, from all eternity, give a people to be his seed, and to be by him in time redeemed, called, justified, sanctified, and glorified.[11]

Blessed Assurance, Jesus Is Mine
In the previous chapter, I wrote of my battle with sin and the many trials I faced to find assurance that my sins were truly forgiven. Countless hours were passed on my knees, or totally prostrate on the ground, confessing sin and abhorring my own self. There were even times where I simply prayed that if the Lord had not pardoned me and would not wash away my sin, that He would strike me dead instead. (The fact that I now live is a testimony unto His sovereign grace and His willingness to forgive, cleanse, and save sinners.)

For years, I wondered if I would ever have any degree of assurance. Would I ever, without pride, be able to say that I knew I was saved? Eventually, the Lord graciously trained my eyes to stop looking to myself and to begin looking to Christ. Once my eyes were set on Him, I learned to trust the greatness of the salvation He had purchased at Calvary.

I have already written how Martin Luther's explanation of Romans 1:17 brought me the greatest peace in my battle with sin.

---

11. The Savoy Declaration (8.1), Reformed Standards, accessed December 2, 2023, https://reformedstandards.com/british/savoy.html.

Romans 1:17, I believe, also offers great comfort to those saints facing the affliction of a lack of assurance: "For therein is the righteousness of God revealed from faith to faith: as it is written, The just shall live by faith." The faith that justifies is the same faith by which we live the Christian life. It is the faith by which we grip hold of Christ. The need to find assurance is great, but if we possess Christ, we have something greater than our need. To quote Thomas Adam, "I can say truly, I have a great need of Christ; thank God, I can say boldly, I have a great Christ for my need."[12]

Allow me to reiterate this once more since we are so prone to forget it: we are justified by faith, and so it is faith alone that can bring about the surest and truest sense of Christian assurance. When we recognize it is the object of our faith—Jesus—that saves, we can have the comfort of genuine assurance. It is Jesus who both saves and preserves. Thomas Brooks, reflecting on this great assurance, wrote,

> Christ is to be answerable for all those that are given to Him, at the last day, and therefore we need not doubt but that He will certainly employ all the power of His Godhead to secure and save all those that He must be accountable for. Christ's charge and care of these that are given to Him, extends even to the very day of their resurrection, that He may not so much as lose their dust, but gather it together again, and raise it up in glory to be a proof of His fidelity; for, saith He, "I shall lose nothing, but raise it up again at the last day."[13]

When Satan tempts us to doubt, we can answer, "Yes, I know my faith is weak, my sins great, and my status lowly. What of it? Christ is greater than all this still, and He has promised me my salvation in Him is secure."

When the World opposes us and questions our assurance, we may answer, "I am the chief of sinners, but it just so happens that Jesus is

---

12. Thomas Adam, *Private Thoughts on Religion; Extracted from the Diary of the Rev. Thomas Adam Rector of Wintringham* (London: A. J. Valpy, Red Lion Court, Fleet Street, 1821), 20.

13. Thomas Brooks, *Paradise Opened*, in *The Complete Works of Thomas Brooks* (Edinburgh: James Nichol, 1867), 5:368.

in the business of saving the worst of the worst and lowest of the low. My salvation in Him is secure."

When the flesh attempts to deceive us, we can answer, "Self, what do you know of the power of Christ? Are you God? Are you the judge of salvation? Christ alone is judge; nay, more so, Christ alone is Savior and Christ alone has power to save. I am His, and He is mine. My salvation in Him is secure."

The battle for assurance can be weary and the war long. But how sweet it is to finally grasp the knowledge that we are Christ's and He is ours! John Owen got to the heart of the matter when he wrote,

> Some men have no peace, because they have that without which it is impossible they should have peace. Because they cannot but condemn themselves, they cannot entertain a sense that God doth acquit them. But this is the mystery of the gospel, which unbelief is a stranger unto; nothing but faith can give a real subsistence unto these things in the same soul, at the same time. It is easy to learn the notion of it, but it is not easy to experience the power of it. For a man to have a sight of that within him which would condemn him, for which he is troubled, and at the same time to have a discovery of that without him which will justify him, and to rejoice therein, is that which he is not led unto but by faith in the mystery of the gospel. We are now under a law for justification which excludes all boasting, Rom. iii. 27; so that though we have joy enough in another, yet we may have, we always have, sufficient cause of humiliation in ourselves. The gospel will teach a man to feel sin and believe righteousness at the same time. Faith will carry heaven in one hand and hell in the other; showing the one deserved, the other purchased. A man may see enough of his own sin and folly to bring…a hell of wrath out of heaven; and yet see Christ bring…a heaven of blessedness out of a hell of punishment.[14]

Dear saint, your battle with sin is far from over. The temptations will continue until that time appointed by God when we will forever be in the presence of Christ. The trials will continue. But this much

---

14. Owen, *Exposition upon Psalm CXXX*, 6:547.

is sure: we are saved, and no amount of temptation, trial, or sin will ever separate us from the love of God that we have in Christ Jesus our Lord (Rom. 8:31–39). Our triumphant victory has been assured us by Christ Himself. "The God of peace shall bruise Satan under your feet shortly. The grace of our Lord Jesus Christ be with you. Amen" (Rom. 16:20).

As we fight for faith and assurance, we must never neglect prayer. Prayer is one of our main tools in this battle, and it allows us to directly communicate with God. Personally, I've discovered that when I'm feeling most tempted to doubt and cast myself into despair, praying to the Lord is one of the surest ways to be spiritually reinvigorated. The Puritans knew the power of prayer so well that they were sometimes prone to break out in prayer in the middle of their sermons. Below you'll find a prayer that I've adapted from the writings of John Flavel, and I trust that it will be an encouragement as we seek the face of God:

> Lord, the condemnation was thine,
>   that the justification might be mine;
> The agony thine,
>   that the victory might be mine;
> The pain was thine,
>   and the ease mine;
> The stripes thine,
>   and the healing balm issuing from them mine;
> The vinegar and gall were thine,
>   that the honey and sweet might be mine.
> The curse was thine,
>   that the blessing might be mine;
> The crown of thorns was thine,
>   that the crown of glory might be mine;
> The death was thine,
>   the life purchased by it mine.
> Thou paidst the price
>   that I might enjoy the inheritance.
> I praise you for the great salvation you wrought in me.

Kill this remaining sin, lest it kill me instead.
Carry me through this trial, for I am weary of the battle.
But I look to you and, in hope, trust the victory you bought.
Amen.[15]

Study Questions

1. Do you currently have assurance of salvation? Why or why not? What must you do to attain assurance?

2. Why is a lack of assurance so harmful to the vitality of the Christian life?

3. Consider once more Isaiah 53:2–11. How can this passage become a source of comfort to the saint battling for assurance?

4. Richard Sibbes wrote, "As the strongest faith may be shaken, so the weakest, where truth is, is so far rooted that it will prevail." If it is not the size or amount of faith that a person possesses that brings assurance, then what does?

5. Consider once more the doctrine of adoption and John Owen's rules for attaining assurance. Which of these rules, or doctrines, do you find most comforting? Which do you struggle with the most? What can you do to begin to follow Owen's counsel now?

---

15. This prayer has been adapted from John Flavel's sermon "The Solemn Consecration of the Mediator," in *The Fountain of Life Opened Up: or, A Display of Christ in His Essential and Mediatorial Glory*, in *The Works of John Flavel* (repr., Edinburgh: Banner of Truth, 2021), 1:101. The final four lines are my own.

Chapter 3

Remembering God's Sovereignty When the World Spins Out of Control

The story of Joseph is striking. When we first meet him, he is clearly the beloved of his father, Jacob. Gifted with a coat of many colors, Joseph is almost immediately despised by his brothers. When he shares a series of dreams that entail his entire family bowing before him as their ruler, the anger of his siblings only increases. Though the story starts with Joseph in a high and elevated position, it does not take long for things to turn on their head.

Eventually, we find Joseph being sold into slavery in Egypt. His brothers, completely fed up with the favor that was granted to their younger brother by God, consider how they can get rid of him. First, they think of leaving him alone in a hole in the ground. But upon seeing some slave traders approach, they realize they can sell their brother into slavery. Then all they must do is lie to their father that he was torn apart by lions.

Once Joseph is in Egypt, things go from bad to worse. His master's wife attempts to seduce him, but he flees from the sin. Before he can flee, she is able to grab ahold of his cloak. When her husband returns, she lies and claims that Joseph tried to rape her. It is not long until Joseph is in prison.

While in prison, he is taken advantage of by the jailer, who basically makes Joseph do his job for him. When Joseph correctly interprets the dreams of some of Pharoah's servants, he is neglected once more and forgotten when they are freed.

As time passes, we may begin to ask, Why is God permitting these things to take place? Joseph has done no wrong. Why such hardship?

Why all the trials? Surely, in some sense, Joseph must have pondered the same things. Why all this suffering?

The answer, ultimately, does not come until much later in the book of Genesis. By the time Joseph is finally recognized by Pharoah as a great man of God, exalted to a place of honor, and has saved many peoples from a great famine across the world, one almost forgets about the evils that have befallen him. He is even restored to his family and is able to see his father once more before his death. It is at this point that we have an answer to the question, Why did God permit this evil and suffering?

Joseph's brothers fear that, with their father dead, their younger brother will finally seek his retribution. Would he not be just in doing so? After suffering so much through the years because of their sinful actions in selling him into slavery, would he not have the right to vindicate himself before them with some cruel and unusual punishment? Yet Joseph proves himself once again more righteous than they, for he harbored no such secret machinations of vengeance. Rather, looking at his brothers and remembering the evil that befell him, he tells them, "But as for you, ye thought evil against me; but God meant it unto good, to bring to pass, as it is this day, to save much people alive" (Gen. 50:20).

Joseph recognized one of the most important truths that any Christian can realize: God is able to take every circumstance—even those that others have meant for evil against us—and use them for the greatest good. This is, after all, the basis of Romans 8:28: "And we know that all things work together for good to them that love God, to them who are the called according to his purpose." God is truly working all things for our greatest good and His greatest glory—especially when things seem like they are spiraling out of control.

Looking to Christ in the Chaos
One major question that every Christian must ask is where we will look to when our world spins out of control. Every one of us, at one point or another, will experience disheartening times when, almost without warning, things fall apart. As the old poem goes, "The best

laid plans of mice and men often go awry." What will you do when things go awry?

For the Puritans, the answer was simple: they would look to Christ. It was Christ who orchestrated and ordained all the events that came to pass in their lives. Whether they encountered good or bad, they turned to Christ. He was not only the author and finisher of their faith but the very sustainer of that faith. If there was any comfort to be found, any peace to be had, any joy to be encountered amid great tribulation and trials, they knew it was to be found in Christ. Consider their confessions.

The confessions and catechisms formed during and after the Protestant Reformation contain some of the greatest theological truths that any Christian has ever compiled. The Puritans were, in many ways, master craftsmen when it came to systematizing gospel truths for the good of the church at large. As such, these confessions and catechisms often act as systematic theologies for the average churchgoer and learned theologian alike. These are truths we can learn as children and still delight in at the end of life. Like learning psalms and hymns that stick with us throughout our lives, confessions and catechisms contain pithy and succinct truths that will carry us through the day of suffering and battle.

Of these confessions and creeds, the Heidelberg Catechism may be the most theologically awe-inspiring and comforting of all. In Question and Answer 28, the catechism states this about finding comfort in Christ and His providential hands of care:

> Question 28: What advantage is it to us to know that God has created, and by his providence does still uphold all things?
>
> Answer: That we may be patient in adversity; thankful in prosperity; and that in all things, which may hereafter befall us, we place our firm trust in our faithful God and Father, that nothing shall separate us from his love; since all creatures are so in his hand, that without his will they cannot so much as move.[1]

---

1. Heidelberg Catechism (Q&A 28), Christian Classics Ethereal Library, accessed December 2, 2023, https://www.ccel.org/creeds/heidelberg-cat.html.

What great truths! We are to be *patient* in adversity and *thankful* in prosperity precisely because we know the God who holds all things in His hands. Just as He "turneth [the heart of the king] whithersoever he will" (Prov. 21:1), so too will He turn our lives as He ordains. As Samuel Rodigast wrote in his famous hymn,

> Whate'er my God ordains is right:
> His holy will abideth;
> I will be still, whate'er he doth,
> And follow where he guideth.
> He is my God; though dark my road,
> He holds me that I shall not fall:
> Wherefore to him I leave it all.[2]

The Christian can know the calming comfort of Christ's providence through the knowledge that God has ordained all that comes to pass. There will never be a moment wherein something occurs that causes God to arise from His throne in heaven and pace about, scratching His head, while wondering what to do next. Nothing will ever catch Him by surprise, for He knows, sees, and ordains (or sovereignly permits) all. If evil occurs, it is because God has permitted it for a good purpose. If good occurs, it is because God has ordained it for a good purpose. All that happens is according to His sovereign providence, and we can trust Him to accomplish good through all.

Samuel Willard, the New England Puritan born in Concord, Massachusetts, recognized these great truths as well. He knew that the Christian finds the deepest joy, even in trials, in the recognition of Christ and His providential goodness, which orders all things. Reflecting on the ways in which most men are quick to label their days evil according to their circumstances, Willard recognized that of all the ways in which the Christian is most comforted in this world, it is the presence of Christ Himself that best comforts the wearied saint:

---

2. Samuel Rodigast, "Whate'er My God Ordains Is Right, Holy His Will Abideth," Hymnary.org, accessed November 21, 2023, https://hymnary.org/text/whateer_my_god_ordains_is_right_holy_his.

Everyone is ready to make his remarks on the times that he lives in, and which pass over him, and to judge of them whether the days are good or evil. The generality of men take their measures from the observation of outward Providence. If there be outward peace and plenty, they call them happy days; if outward distress and trouble, they call them evil. But we have a better rule, and more safe for Christians, and that is to judge according as this fountain is opened amongst us. The more of Christ that a people enjoy, the happier are they, and the less he is known and acknowledged in his great design of Mediatorship, the greater is the infelicity of such a people.[3]

Those who do not find comfort in the sovereignty of God have not rightly understood what the sovereignty of God entails. The fact that our triune God holds all things in His hands should bring immense comfort to all His people precisely because "every good gift and every perfect gift is from above, and cometh down from the Father of lights, with whom is no variableness, neither shadow of turning" (James 1:17).

The Comfort of Sovereign Providence and Predestination

Over the years, I've read a lot of books that may be considered classics. I read new books as well, but I gravitate toward older literature. Some of these works contain what some have described as *purple prose*—ornate and elaborate sentences that use fanciful language when simple language would do just as well. Some of it sounds just plain strange to our modern ears. But there are, I think, some great insights from even the fiction writings of the past. Take, for example, the following quote from Herman Melville's magnum opus, *Moby-Dick*: "Ha! ha! ha! ha! hem! clear my throat!—I've been thinking over it ever since, and that ha, ha's the final consequence. Why so? Because a laugh's the wisest, easiest answer to all that's queer; and come what will, one comfort's always left—that unfailing comfort is,

---

3. Samuel Willard, *The Fountain Opened: or, The Great Gospel Priviledge of Having Christ Exhibited to Sinfull Men* (Boston, Mass.: B. Green and J. Allen, for Samuel Sewall Junior, 1700), 123.

it's all predestinated.... I know not all that may be coming, but be it what it will, I'll go to it laughing."[4]

Moby-Dick is a fascinating book. It contains what R. C. Sproul thought to be one of the greatest sermons ever preached on the book of Jonah. It is filled to the brim with theological meaning, and hardly a page goes by without some philosophical meandering. That's not even mentioning the *very* in-depth and descriptive accounts of whaling (which is probably when most people give up on the book entirely). But it's this strange section in chapter 39 that has stuck with me the most.

In this short chapter, attention is turned to the character Stubb, one of the *Pequod*'s (the whaling ship's) three mates. Stubb is a bit fatalistic and sees no reason to wrestle fate. He's been whaling so long that the threat of the whale or even of death puts no fear in him. So, when faced with the possibility of battling a behemoth creature, uncertainty, worries, and possible death, his response is to laugh. And laugh heartily at that.

Though he laughs for the wrong reasons (life is not fatalistic) and finds joy in a misunderstanding of what predestination consists of (it's not blind indifference that orchestrates our lives, but the providence of a caring God), he has things in common with the Puritans, and, as such, there are some things we can learn from his character today.

We Can Find Comfort in All That Has Been Predestinated by Our God
Again, we must highlight the truth that Stubb missed: providence is not the unseeing and uncaring plight thrust on us by an unknowing *indifference* but rather the careful and lovingly ordained plans of our sovereign God to bring about goodness in our lives and glory to His name.

God's Word is replete with promises that He has predestined all that comes to pass. Consider, for example, Ephesians 1:3–12 and its language about predestination coupled with great assurance to the saint and the promise of God receiving glory:

---

[4]. Herman Melville, *Moby-Dick: Or the Whale* (New York: Tor Classics, 1996), 179.

> Blessed be the God and Father of our Lord Jesus Christ, who hath blessed us with all spiritual blessings in heavenly places in Christ: according as he hath chosen us in him before the foundation of the world, that we should be holy and without blame before him in love: having predestinated us unto the adoption of children by Jesus Christ to himself, according to the good pleasure of his will, to the praise of the glory of his grace, wherein he hath made us accepted in the beloved. In whom we have redemption through his blood, the forgiveness of sins, according to the riches of his grace; wherein he hath abounded toward us in all wisdom and prudence; having made known unto us the mystery of his will, according to his good pleasure which he hath purposed in himself: that in the dispensation of the fulness of times he might gather together in one all things in Christ, both which are in heaven, and which are on earth; even in him: in whom also we have obtained an inheritance, being predestinated according to the purpose of him who worketh all things after the counsel of his own will: that we should be to the praise of his glory, who first trusted in Christ.

Notice in verse 3 that God the Father is to be blessed because He has *blessed us* with every spiritual blessing in Christ. From where do these blessings originate? According to verse 4, these spiritual blessings spring forth from God having chosen—or elected—us to salvation from before the foundation of the world. In verse 5, we understand that our election unto salvation in Christ finds its origin in the providential decrees of God. Again, we are told to praise God in verse 6 because, in verses 7–9, He has revealed to us the mystery and wisdom of salvation in Christ.

Then, in verses 10 and 11, we learn that we have been predestinated, by His will, to obtain the inheritance of spiritual blessings in Christ so that Christ Himself would be glorified above all else. All this God has done as the One "who worketh all things after the counsel of his own will." And what is the end goal of all these great and wonderful truths? That God would again receive glory from our lives, which He Himself has ordained (v. 12)!

We Can Meet Adversity with Hearty Laughter Because
We Trust God's Providence

Because we trust in God and His divine providence directing our lives, we can meet our trials with a hearty dose of laughter, knowing that "the joy of the LORD is [our] strength" (Neh. 8:10). Thomas Watson taught on this in his magisterial *A Body of Divinity*, in which he wrote elegantly of God's providence. Like the apostle Paul in Romans 9, Watson preemptively assumes the questions of his readers:

> Some say, There are many things done in the world which are very disorderly and irregular; and surely God's providence is not in these things.
>
> Yes, the things that seem to us irregular, God makes use of to his own glory. Suppose you were in a smith's shop, and should see there several sorts of tools, some crooked, some bowed, others hooked, would you condemn all these things, because they do not look handsome? The smith makes use of them all for doing his work. Thus it is with the providences of God; they seem to us to be very crooked and strange, yet they all carry on God's work. I shall make this clear to you in two particular cases.[5]

Watson goes on to explain that even when the saints of God are cast down very low, or when the wicked seem to flourish, yet "God is to be trusted [even] when his providences seem to run contrary to his promises."[6] Indeed, he says that God's providence is so very vital that

> the providence of God keeps the whole creation upon the wheels, or else it would soon be dissolved, and the very axletree would break in pieces. If God's providence should be withdrawn but for a while, creatures would be dissolved, and run into their first nothing. Without this wise providence of God there would be anxiety and confusion in the whole world, just like an army when it is routed and scattered. The providence of God infuses comfort and virtue into everything we enjoy. Our clothes would not warm us, our food would not nourish us, without the

---

5. Thomas Watson, *A Body of Divinity* (1692; repr., Edinburgh: Banner of Truth, 1965), 121.

6. Watson, *Body of Divinity*, 123.

special providence of God. And does not all this deserve your admiration of providence?[7]

We Can Trust God's Providence Even When We Do Not Understand What He Is Doing

The promises of Genesis 50:20 and Romans 8:28 ring true all throughout Scripture: God is able to use even evil in a nonevil way to accomplish our greatest good and His greatest glory. Thomas Goodwin noted this very thing when, writing on Ephesians, he explained,

> If you have any privilege in grace above another, it dependeth upon predestination, as well as your salvation doth; it dependeth upon an act of God's eternal love. The Apostle, as he ascribed their salvation to predestination, so this privilege, that they first trusted in Christ; it was ordered by the counsel of God's everlasting will, "being predestinated," saith he, "who first trusted in Christ." Therefore, not only have recourse to bless God and his eternal decrees for his love in saving thee, but for any particular privilege that thou hast before others in point of grace; have recourse to God's eternal counsel, for it was the fountain of it, as well of the degrees of grace as of glory; they have all their spring from God's eternal decree, as well as who shall be saved and who not.[8]

All the graces we receive in Christ, from salvation to provision, are ours because of God's divine predestination. All the trials we receive that strengthen us and mold us to the image of Christ are ours due to God's permitting them in His sovereign predestination of all things.

Seeing God's Caring Providence in Trials

One of my favorite quotes from any Puritan comes from Samuel Rutherford. He was writing a letter to a young Christian when he penned these words: "Your heart is not the compass Christ saileth by. He will give you leave to sing as you please, but he will not dance to

---

7. Watson, *Body of Divinity*, 124.
8. Thomas Goodwin, *An Exposition of the Epistle to the Ephesians*, in *The Works of Thomas Goodwin* (Eureka, Calif.: Tanski Publications, 1996), 1:222.

your tune. It is not referred to you and your thoughts, what Christ will do with the charters betwixt you and him. Your own misbelief hath torn them, but he hath the principle in heaven with himself. Your thoughts are no parts of the new covenant; dreams change not Christ."[9]

Our thoughts and dreams do not change Christ. He does not navigate according to the compass of our heart (feelings). His promises and providential purposes prove true, even when everything else seems to fall apart. We can trust God's purposes even when we don't understand what's happening.

As a minister of the gospel, I am no stranger to trials. Often, the same sheep I am attempting to care for and feed with the Word are the very ones biting me. As I do my best to chase them back into the sheepfold, to protect them from wolves, they cartoonishly walk into the open jaws of beasts waiting idly by.

Some time ago, I found myself under quite a fiery trial. I was working alongside another minister, one I counted as a great friend, who had requested to join us in planting a church. He was looking to leave the church he was serving at for several reasons but wanted to find a place to continue serving. Our church was about two months into the work of getting established in the community when he contacted me about joining. On paper, it seemed a great fit. He claimed to hold to the Second London Baptist Confession of Faith, agreed with expository preaching, and loved the idea of family-integrated worship (where families worship together rather than sending the children away during the worship service to a children's church), and all three of those things were major staples of our church's vision. What seemed only a few days later, he had quit his church, and the pressure was on to speed up the process of making him an elder. Though this should have been a red flag, I was young and trusted that he had the best interest of the church and the glory of God at heart. Besides, he was over a decade older than me, and I truly believed he was a great friend.

---

9. Rutherford, *Letters of Samuel Rutherford*, 350.

When he first came to the church, he brought over a hundred people with him. It was then that it dawned on me that a church split had occurred at his previous church. I was worried but still hoped to make it work. Mere weeks passed, however, before he and a large portion of this new congregation turned against both me and aspects of Reformed theology. The more I tried to reason with them to not neglect the glorious truths we had been given to treasure and cherish in Scripture, the more he and they seemed to distance themselves from me. They soon stopped speaking with me. When I preached, some would not attend or would actively complain, "You're too professional, and this is a rural community.... He resonates with us, but you don't.... We want to hear him, not you." Complaints about the music began too. "We don't want to sing Psalms.... We want the songs we used to sing.... We want the old hymns." Even complaints about the building were being uttered. "This school doesn't *feel* like a church." It seemed there would be no pleasing anyone.

I was admittedly hurt by the sizable number of people who disliked me and complained about me. Yet Rutherford's words rang true: My heart is not the compass Christ sails by. I had to trust God.

It was clear, though, that things were not going well. But I was embarrassed to openly admit this. I had agreed to this man joining us, and I was the driving force behind having him voted in as an elder. When I spoke with other pastors, almost every one of them said that they would *never* have originally counseled me to permit him to join our elder team. This only made me feel worse as I realized the problem was of my own making. It felt like I was being told, "You got yourself into this mess. Now you must get yourself out."

I was ashamed of my mistakes, but the shame would soon worsen. A few weeks after the complaints against me began, rumors also started to spread about me in the community, which seemed to be propagated from all over. "He's a cult leader," they said of me, "because he doesn't believe that *only* the King James Bible is the inspired and preserved Word of God. He thinks we should sing *psalms*. Also, he teaches Calvinism. And Calvinism *is* a cult." Such charges hardly seemed to be worthy of a defense, so foolish they appeared at first sight. After all, how could any of these things make me a cult leader? But, oh, how I had underestimated the terrible depths of wickedness in the hearts of sinful men.

We were a confessional church holding to the 1689 Second London Baptist Confession of Faith, and we admitted this publicly. We boldly proclaimed that our singing would be congregational, biblically sound, and would focus on learning the Psalms—something that had rarely, if ever, been attempted in our rural community. And while it is true that I believe there are a few English translations of the Scriptures that are acceptable, I still love the King James Bible—along with the English Standard Version and New American Standard Bible. I also love to read the Hebrew and Greek manuscripts for greater clarity and understanding. Could people truly resent a minister of the gospel for doing these things? Besides, there was no denying what I *actually* believed and taught, or what the church professed. All one had to do was listen to my sermons or read one of my articles, and it would have been exceptionally clear that I hold to Reformed theology.

But, as these things often do, the rumors caught fire and spread. "Have you heard," others in the community began to say now, "about *that* pastor? I heard he's teaching a false doctrine called *Calvinism*." Now, the truth was, I absolutely was teaching Calvinism. I still do. Our doctrinal standards say that our church is Calvinistic and Reformed. I adamantly oppose the claim, however, that Calvinism, or Reformed theology, is a cult. It's a shockingly brazen statement to make that is utterly foolish upon inspection. Calvinism is merely the name that was given to the system of Reformed theology that is thoroughly biblical, orthodox, and historical.

To make a long story short, the man whom I was working with agreed it was best that he leave our church. When he did, he took a sizable portion of the congregation with him to start another church. Even some who were with us in the first few months before he joined left to follow him. This was a new challenge. For the next few weeks, I would drive by and see their meeting place, the parking lot filled with cars, as I made my way to the high school we were meeting at, with ten to fifteen cars parked outside. I don't hold this against him—it simply was not a good fit. But it did create a lot of hurt and challenge that could otherwise have been avoided.

It really felt like things had spiraled out of control, and it was my fault for not being wiser. I was embarrassed, especially when people from other churches would ask me what had happened. It felt like my back had become a target for the knives of others, but I knew it was my own fault for being rash in appointing an elder. Rumors were spreading about me and the church, a mass exodus of churchgoers was occurring, and I wasn't sure how we were going to afford rent for our small number of congregants, let alone how the needs of my family would be met.

Yet Rutherford's words rang true once more: my heart is not the compass Christ sails by. I had to trust God's promises and providential purposes.

My experience during the months that followed proved the words of Joseph true: "Ye thought evil against me; but God meant it unto good" (Gen. 50:20). Romans 8:28 was also a constant source of encouragement: "And we know that all things work together for good to them that love God, to them who are the called according to his purpose." What I thought would be our ruin actually brought our remaining church body closer together. We learned to weep, laugh, trust God, and pray together. God used this time to strengthen us and His church by pruning out that which would keep us from growing as He had ordained.

Waiting and Hoping in the Providential Hands of God

If we can learn anything from our trials and those of the Puritans, it is this: God does not promise that we will not suffer as Christians, but He does promise to orchestrate the events of our lives—both good and bad—in such a way that our greatest good and His greatest glory will always be accomplished.

We must learn, like Joseph, to trust God's good purposes even when things seem to be falling apart. The same God who said to the sea, "Hitherto shalt thou come, but no further: and here shall thy proud waves be stayed" (Job 38:11) is the same God who holds back our trials and tribulations from consuming us.

As we go through trials, our waiting can be filled with a great deal of hope precisely because we know that Christ will be triumphant in time and space because of His providential purposes. The children's hymn says, "He's got the whole world in His hands." When things seem to fall apart, He is the One holding it together and orchestrating events as He pleases. We must not confuse what we feel with what God is actually doing. Our feelings are uncertain, and they ebb and flow with the tides of change. But remember: our hearts are not the compass Christ sails by.

Jonathan Edwards knew well the sovereignty of God. Below you will find one of his prayers, which is contained within Iain Murray's biography of him. It will, I believe, help us to find greater solace in the God who truly does have the whole world in His hands:

> First of all, I give and commend my soul into the hands of God that gave it, and to the Lord Jesus Christ its glorious, all-sufficient, faithful and chosen Redeemer, relying alone on the free and infinite mercy and grace of God through His worthiness and mediation, for its eternal salvation; and my body I commend to the earth, to be committed to the dust in decent Christian burial…hoping, through the grace, faithfulness and almighty power of my everlasting Redeemer, to receive the same again, at the last day, made like unto His glorious body.[10] Amen.

---

10. Iain H. Murray, *Jonathan Edwards: A New Biography* (Edinburgh: Banner of Truth, 1987), 422.

Study Questions
1. Read Genesis 37–50. In what ways was God directing Joseph's life when things seemed to be out of control?

2. What is the providence of God, and what comfort may be drawn from this doctrine?

3. What lessons can we learn about providence—both good and bad—from the character Stubb in *Moby-Dick*?

4. Samuel Rutherford wrote that our hearts are not the compasses whereby Christ sails. What does this mean for us when things seem to be falling apart?

5. God is sovereignly reigning over all things. As we wait and hope, what comfort should this bring?

Chapter 4

Following the One Who Endured the Cross, Despising Its Shame

Beaten, ridiculed, mocked, stripped, and crucified, our bruised and bloodied Savior hung, naked and nailed to a wooden cross. Above His head hung a sign reading, "THIS IS JESUS THE KING OF THE JEWS" (Matt. 27:37). This was meant to degrade rather than honor Him. The crowd played their part in humiliating Him too, mocking Him by shouting, "He saved others; himself he cannot save. If he be the King of Israel, let him now come down from the cross, and we will believe him. He trusted in God; let him deliver him now, if he will have him: for he said, I am the Son of God" (Matt. 27:42–43). As they jeered and laughed, they failed to see the glorious truth that this man who hung bleeding before them like a criminal was truly the perfect, sinless, spotless, and righteous Son of God.

Could there have been any greater humiliation hurled at our Lord and Savior than this? Could there have been any greater shame? If it was shameful for Noah's sons to uncover and see his nakedness, resulting in a curse (Gen. 9:21–27), how much worse of an offense was it for the Creator to be stripped and killed by His creation?

Yet, as shameful and humiliating as His death was, it cannot be stripped of its glory. This was not a humiliating death with no purpose behind it; this was the most important death that anyone has ever died, for it was *the* death that defeated death! Jesus would later exclaim to John, "I am he that liveth, and was dead; and, behold, I am alive for evermore, Amen; and have the keys of hell and of death" (Rev. 1:18). Truly, Jesus has the right to say, "I am the resurrection, and the life: he that believeth in me, though he were dead, yet shall he live: and whosoever liveth and believeth in me shall never die" (John 11:25-26), precisely because "having spoiled principalities and powers [through His death on the cross and subsequent resurrection], he made a shew of them openly, triumphing over them in it" (Col. 2:15). He suffered and endured the humiliation because He knew the endgame: glory, honor, and praise for Himself, and eternal life for His elect.

As the writer of Hebrews put it, we must be found, especially in suffering and trials, "looking unto Jesus the author and finisher of our faith; who for the joy that was set before him endured the cross, despising the shame, and is set down at the right hand of the throne of God. For consider him that endured such contradiction of sinners against himself, lest ye be wearied and faint in your minds. Ye have not yet resisted unto blood, striving against sin" (12:2-4).

Philippians 2:5-11 is similar. It is a famous portion of Scripture that was probably originally sung as a hymn in the early church. In it, the apostle Paul urges the saints to model their lives after Christ. He writes,

> Let this mind be in you, which was also in Christ Jesus: who, being in the form of God, thought it not robbery to be equal with God: but made himself of no reputation, and took upon him the form of a servant, and was made in the likeness of men: and being found in fashion as a man, he humbled himself, and became obedient unto death, even the death of the cross. Wherefore God also hath highly exalted him, and given him a name which is above every name: that at the name of Jesus every knee should bow, of things in heaven, and things in earth, and things under the earth; and that every tongue should confess that Jesus Christ is Lord, to the glory of God the Father.

This Jesus, who humbled Himself to serve sinners and embraced shame and humiliation to accomplish the salvation of His people, is our example. In fact, the slave cannot expect better than the Master received (John 13:16). If Jesus suffered humiliation, then we must expect to suffer much the same.

But suffering humiliation on behalf of Christ is truly no shame at all. It comes with a most glorious promise that, one day, "at the name of Jesus every knee should bow, of things in heaven, and things in earth, and things under the earth; and that every tongue should confess that Jesus Christ is Lord, to the glory of God the Father." His victory is our victory.

The gloriously good news for the saints is that when shame, humiliation, and other trials like them come, we can rest in the assurance that we are not fighting *for* victory. Rather, we are fighting *from within* the victory that is ours in Jesus Christ.

Encountering Humiliation and Shame with the Puritans

If ever there was one group of Christians that had to regularly endure humiliation and shame from the hands of sinful men, it was the Puritans. The name itself was meant to bring reproach. Traditional members of the Church of England (Anglicans) had resisted the desire of the Puritans to keep reforming the church from the inside out, those who desired to *purify* the Church of England by distancing it further from Roman Catholic practices, like the minister's wearing of vestments. This became known as the vestiarian controversy and gave rise to the derogatory use of the term *Puritan*. Nick Needham explains,

> The vestiarian controversy (as it was called) was the occasion when the term "Puritan" was first used as an abusive label for the Anglican dissidents. It was also around the same time that Puritanism showed its potential for Separatism. In June 1567 in London, the sheriff's officers (the 16th century police) uncovered a group of a hundred holding a meeting in Plumbers' Hall, allegedly for a wedding—but they had in reality gathered to listen to preaching and take part in holy communion. Arrested and questioned by Bishop Grindal of London, the replies made it clear that this was a functional congregation. They had met in secret as Protestants during Mary Tudor's reign. Disillusioned, however, with what they saw as the insufficiently Protestant character of the Elizabethan Anglican Church, most of whose ministers (they said) were mere papists who had conformed to

the 1559 settlement, they had decided to resume meeting as a Protestant congregation outside the establishment.[1]

The arrests would, of course, continue and Puritan persecution would culminate nearly a century later in the Great Ejection of 1662. But the centuries following have proved to be unkind to their memory as well, and modernity has not been sympathetic to the Puritans either.

While it is true that Christians returned to the writings of the Puritans in the second half of the twentieth century with renewed passion and vigor, finding within their theology a thoroughly Reformed, experiential, and pastoral warmth nearly impossible to replicate elsewhere, secularism continued to wag its disgruntled, boney finger at these old saints. Perhaps the most famous anecdotal statement against them comes from the pen of H. L. Mencken, who mockingly wrote, "Puritanism—The haunting fear that someone, somewhere, may be happy."[2] (One may respond that "secularism is the joyless fear that Christians are right and pagans are wrong," and one would be wonderfully right in doing so.)

It seems to be a reoccurring truth that the more holy and righteous one lives on this earth, the more this world will try its best to tear that person down through humiliating tactics and shameful strategies. As the writer of Hebrews faithfully records of past saints, "And others had trial of cruel mockings and scourgings, yea, moreover of bonds and imprisonment: they were stoned, they were sawn asunder, were tempted, were slain with the sword: they wandered about in sheepskins and goatskins; being destitute, afflicted, tormented; (of whom the world was not worthy:) they wandered in deserts, and in mountains, and in dens and caves of the earth" (11:36–38). The kingdom of darkness has always attempted to wage war against the citizens of the kingdom of light. It should be no surprise to discover that the humiliation and shame we endure as Christians at the hand of sinners has been normative for the life of the church.

---

1. Nick Needham, *2000 Years of Christ's Power* (Fearn, Scotland: Christian Focus, 2016), 4:185–86.

2. Henry Louis Mencken, *A Mencken Chrestomathy* (1949; repr., New York: Alfred A. Knopf, 1967), 624.

While examples abound, perhaps there is no better illustration of Puritan triumph through suffering and humiliation than the life of Cotton Mather. Most famous today for his involvement in the Salem Witch Trials, Mather is unjustly neglected by most Christians and unfairly remembered as a racist and misogynistic bigot. While the centuries have certainly been unkind to Mather, his own day often proved to be just as humiliating and cruel.

Most of these rumors of misogyny and wickedness were propagated by an enemy of Mather, the merchant Robert Calef. Dustin Benge and Nate Pickowicz explain that Calef, "while a respected man in his own right, believed that Cotton was exploiting the witchcraft trials for his own notoriety."[3] Admittedly, Mather had published his *Memorable Providences, Relating to Witchcraft and Possessions* in 1689 and *The Wonders of the Invisible World* in 1693, which was understood to be Mather's endorsement of the trials.

However, Benge and Pickowicz expound on the thought of Puritan scholar Perry Miller, who "contends that Cotton had been pressured by Governor William Phips and Lieutenant Governor William Stoughton to write the damning account."[4] Most likely, Cotton was forced to write in favor of the witch trials. In fact, "Most modern historians concur with Miller's assessment that Cotton was 'insecure, frightened, [and] sick at heart' over the whole situation."[5] Whatever the case, Mather was *not* the one who had tried or killed people during the Salem Witch Trials. Yet this did not stop the terrible and humiliating accusations that Calef would make.

In 1700, several years after Mather had published his works on the witch trials, Robert Calef went on to publish *More Wonders of the Invisible World*. Within, "Calef claimed that, during their treatment of a bewitched girl named Margaret Rule, Increase [Cotton's father] and Cotton both sexually assaulted her. Despite dozens of witnesses

---

3. Dustin Benge and Nate Pickowicz, *The American Puritans* (Grand Rapids: Reformation Heritage Books, 2020), 193.
4. Benge and Pickowicz, *American Puritans*, 190.
5. Benge and Pickowicz, *American Puritans*, 191. The quote is taken from Perry Miller, *The New England Mind: From Colony to Province* (Cambridge, Mass.: Harvard University Press, 1953), 201.

present during the alleged misconduct, Calef maintained his uncorroborated story."[6] That was a terribly humiliating allegation against Cotton, which painted him not only as a sexually abusive and deviant man but as one who sought to take advantage of others from within a position of power.

Of course, all this neglects the fact that Mather was astonishingly brilliant. He published the very first American scientific textbook in 1721, *The Christian Philosopher*. He studied just about everything from geology, to zoology, to astronomy, and more. He wrote extensively, keeping a large correspondence with such men as Isaac Newton. To think of Cotton Mather as merely a superstitious, power-hungry, sexually abusive, racist, and misogynistic hypocrite is not only to do a disservice to his memory; it is, quite frankly, wrong.

So, how did Cotton handle the humiliation of allegations against him? What kept the Puritan Pilgrim going? Nothing less than his confident faith that God would turn his trials to rejoicing, his sorrows to laughter, and his humiliation to victory. After the deaths of two wives, an unhappy marriage with a third, and the deaths of twelve of his children, coupled with the humiliating accusations against him, Cotton still penned these words:

> My SAVIOR yett affords me this Light in my Darkness, that He enables me, to offer up all the Sacrifices He calls me to! And as for the continual Dropping which I suffer in my Family, I freely submit and consent unto it, that the Glorious Lord should continue the Sorrows of it upon me all the few remaining Days of my Pilgrimage, and never give me any release until I dy; only lett me obtain this one Thing of Him; a Soul full of a CHRIST! A mind, not only assured of His being my SAVIOUR, but also sensible of His gracious and quickening Influences, and continually irradiated with the precious Thoughts of Him.[7]

When humiliating trials come and deep shame seems poised to win the day, when we are embarrassed by false accusations or by the

---

6. Benge and Pickowicz, *American Puritans*, 192.

7. Cotton Mather, *The Diary of Cotton Mather* (New York: Frederick Ungar, 1911), 2:754. Quoted in Benge and Pickowicz, *American Puritans*, 201.

hatred of our enemies, when we feel the soul-crushing weight of this world's disgrace upon us, let us cry out with Mather our great hope—namely, that Christ is our Savior still! Let us pray, ultimately, for a soul *full* of Christ! This will quickly dispel any notion of shame or reproach from our hearts and souls.

The Humiliating Lows and Exalting Highs of Following Christ

Cotton Mather's troubles and the false accusations against him were extreme, but his humiliation is not exactly peculiar to his own life. Perhaps you can relate to him in many ways. I sure can.

I wrote in the previous chapter about the struggle I and my family endured when planting a church and having rumors about us swirl throughout the community. In many ways, it was a humiliating time. Those who attended other churches in the area had heard one of our elders had left and had heard rumors about what had happened, and they would inevitably ask me questions about what had happened. Each time, I would feel that rush of humiliation come creeping back as I could almost hear the whispered rumors and shameful lies being uttered about me behind my back. It was foolish to be ashamed of their whispers, but it is part of our fallen human nature to desire to be loved and applauded. What a great reminder it is, then, that Jesus actually warned against being loved by man. "Woe unto you, when all men shall speak well of you! for so did their fathers to the false prophets" (Luke 6:26). We may *think* we want the world to love us, but we really don't. If we are children of the Most High God, we must embrace the hatred of this world for what it is: the hatred of sinners for our God.

Incidentally, it was around the same time of my own struggle that I was reintroduced to the story of Jonathan Edwards, which is similar in some ways to Cotton Mather's. A central figure in the First Great Awakening, Edwards had contact with George Whitefield and even experienced amazing revivals himself. But with great highs often come terrible lows, and Edwards experienced both in strides.

While he is perhaps most famous for his sermon "Sinners in the Hands of an Angry God," Edwards wrote several fantastic works on philosophy, theology, and practical ethics. It is not by mistake that he is remembered today as perhaps the greatest intellect that America has ever produced.

However, despite all his intellect and theological fervor, Edwards was no stranger to controversy. He experienced the amazing work of God in spiritual revival in his Northampton church during the fall of 1734. On June 22, 1750, he was dismissed from this church. Imagine the humiliation Edwards and his family were forced to endure at the hands of sinful men!

There are numerous reasons for why he was dismissed from the congregation. Iain Murray has recorded that because of his practice "not 'to visit his people in their own houses unless he was sent for by the sick,' it was inevitable that he should appear more remote and more absorbed in study than is usual among parish ministers. In the eyes of some, he dwelt apart as though he had no time for the common, everyday interests of his people."[8] Whether it was ultimately this or some other perceived fault, he was dismissed from the pastorate and gave his final sermon on July 1, 1751.

Many have heard of how Edwards would then travel to the frontier town of Stockbridge, Massachusetts, and how he ministered to the Native Americans there. However, his troubles were far from over. His troubles from Northampton spilled over into Stockbridge, with some of the same families still opposing his missionary efforts among the Native Americans. They would try to humiliate and shame him further.

The biggest controversy surrounded his operation of a mission school in Stockbridge. The Williams family, from Northampton, seemed to have had a significant disdain for Edwards ever since the Great Awakening had taken place. On this occasion, they had attempted to persuade the governor of Massachusetts, Sir William Pepperrell, to remove Edwards from Stockbridge and to stop his work among the Native Americans at the mission school. Edwards defended himself in a letter to the governor, writing,

---

8. Murray, *Jonathan Edwards*, 342.

I would pray you to consider, Sir, the disadvantage I am under, not knowing [what] has been said against me in conversation, not knowing what to answer to. The ruin of [my] usefulness and the ruin of my poor family (which has greatly suffered in times past for righteousness' sake) are not things of equal consideration with the public good. Yet, certainly, I should first have an equal, impartial, and candid hearing, before I am executed for the public good.[9]

One truly gets the sense of the burdensome trial he was under. Why, one might ask, would God permit the injustices to continue to follow Edwards? Well, as the Lord would have it, these vicious attacks and assaults against Edwards could not stop the work that God had called him to. It seems, to some degree, that God permitted these trials both to strengthen Edwards and to encourage the faith of saints in similar trials: Truly, those who are persecuted for righteousness' sake are most blessed (Matt. 5:10–12).

Around this time, in October 1753, Edwards wrote a letter to Thomas Gillespie outlining some of the trials he was enduring by the grace of God:

As to my own circumstances, I am still meeting with trouble, and expect no other as long as I live in this world. Some great men have mightily opposed my continuing the missionary at Stockbridge, and have taken occasion abundantly to reproach me, and endeavor my removal. But I desire to bless God; he seems in some respects to set me out of their reach. He raises me up friends who are exerting themselves for me in opposition to my enemies; particularly the Commissioners for Indian Affairs in Boston, with whom innumerable artifices have been used, to disaffect them towards me, but altogether in vain. Gov. [Jonathan] Belcher also has seen cause much to exert himself in my behalf on occasion of the opposition made to me. My people, both English and Indians, steadfastly adhere to me,

---

9. Jonathan Edwards, "To Sir William Pepperrell," Jonathan Edwards Center at Yale University, accessed December 2, 2023, http://edwards.yale.edu/archive?path=aHR0cDovL2Vkd2FyZHMueWFsZS5lZHUvY2dpLWJpbi9uZXdwaGlsby9nZXRvYmplY3QucGw/Yy4xNToxNy53amVv.

excepting the family with whom the opposition began and those related to that family, which family greatly opposed me while at Northampton. Most numerous, continual, and indefatigable endeavors have been used to undermine me, by alienating my people from me. Innumerable mean artifices have been used, with one and another, young and old, men and women, Indians and English; but hitherto they have been greatly disappointed. But yet they are not weary.[10]

He knew that the vexing trials against him were many, that his enemies surrounded him, and that Satan desired nothing more than to bring an end to his ministry. Edwards knew his enemies aimed to humiliate him, but he would bear his cross with faith. While it surely must have felt as though the world were spinning out of control, he writes that his fervent desire was yet to praise the Lord. He knew his enemies had been greatly disappointed in their attempts to destroy and humiliate him because the providential hands of God had continued to support him.

Enduring Humiliation with Hope
Edwards knew the providential hand of God in trials well. Writing on Revelation 12:10 ("For the accuser of our brethren is cast down"), he explained that

> God tries the graces of his people by persecutions, that the truth and power of his grace in them may appear to his own glory, both before men, angels and devils. One end is that by such a discovery of the truth and strength of their faith and love, he may as it were triumph over Satan; and make him to see what a victory is obtained over him, by so rescuing those souls that were once his captives from his power; and convince him of the real success of his design of redeeming and sanctifying souls—notwithstanding all that he had done to [them], whereby he

---

10. Jonathan Edwards, "To the Reverend Thomas Gillespie," Jonathan Edwards Center at Yale University, accessed December 2, 2023, http://edwards.yale.edu/archive?path=aHR0cDovL2Vkd2FyZHMueWFsZS5lZHUvY2dpLWJpbi9uZXdwaGlsby9ZXRvYmplY3QucGw/Yy4xNToyMjoxNC53amVv.

thought he had utterly ruined mankind, and put them past the possibility of cure.[11]

Edwards was eventually called to become president of Yale University. While there, he received a failed smallpox vaccine and soon contracted the virus and died. Yet, even in sickness and death, Edwards trusted in God. His physician remarked, "Never...did any mortal man more fully and clearly evidence the sincerity of all his professions, by one continued, universal, calm, cheerful resignation and patient submission to the divine will, through each stage of his disease."[12] What a testimony! What a remarkable body of work! What a life lived unto the glory of God!

This was a man who, ultimately, knew that his life was in the hands of his sovereign God and that God's cause would finally triumph in the world. All the vain attempts of men to shame and humiliate him would, in the final analysis, fail. In his own words, he trusted that

> the Spirit of God shall be gloriously poured out for the wonderful revival and propagation of religion.... This pouring out, when it is begun, shall soon bring great multitudes to forsake that vice and wickedness which now so generally prevails, and shall cause that vital religion, which is now so despised and laughed at in the world, to revive....
>
> The visible kingdom of Satan shall be overthrown and the kingdom of Christ set up on the ruins of it, everywhere throughout the whole habitable globe.[13]

Praise the Lord for the wonderful truth that the realm of Satan's

---

11. Jonathan Edwards, "Notes on the Apocalypse," Jonathan Edwards Center at Yale University, accessed December 2, 2023, http://edwards.yale.edu/archive?path=aHR0cDovL2Vkd2FyZHMueWFsZS5lZHUvY2dpLWJpbi9uZXdwaGlsby9n ZXRvYmplY3QucGw/Yy40OjQud2plby40NjI3NDIuNDYyNzQ3LjQ2MjcOS40Nj I3NTkuNDYyNzYyLjQ2Mjc2Ng==.

12. Quoted in Kenneth D. Macleod, "Jonathan Edwards 7: Stockbridge and Princeton," Banner of Truth, March 16, 2007, https://banneroftruth.org/us/resources/articles/2007/jonathan-edwardssupsupbr7-stockbridge-and-princeton-1/.

13. Quoted in Macleod, "Jonathan Edwards 7: Stockbridge and Princeton." See also Jonathan Edwards, *A History of the Work of Redemption* (repr., Edinburgh: Banner of Truth, 2003), 372–73, 84.

domain will be conquered by Christ's kingdom. Our humiliation will turn to triumph. Our shame will give way to eternal victory. In these truths, we wait and hope and endure the crosses Christ gives us, despising their shame.

One of the great gifts to the church is Arthur Bennett's *The Valley of Vision*. Below I have included a prayer that will help us to put our sinful pride to death, while simultaneously causing us to trust in the Lord to turn our greatest humiliations to triumphant victories:

> O MY LORD AND SAVIOUR,
> You also appointed a cross for me to take up and carry,
> > a cross before You give me a crown.
> You have appointed it to be my portion,
> > but self-love hates it,
> > carnal reason is unreconciled to it;
> > without the grace of patience I cannot bear it,
> > walk with it, profit by it.
> O blessed cross, what mercies do you bring with you!
> You are only esteemed hateful by my rebel will,
> > heavy because I shirk Your load.
> Teach me, gracious Lord and Saviour,
> > that with my cross You send promised grace
> > > so that I may bear it patiently,
> > that my cross is Your yoke which is easy,
> > and Your burden which is light.[14] Amen.

---

14. Arthur Bennett, "The Grace of the Cross," in *The Valley of Vision* (Edinburgh: Banner of Truth, 1975), 172.

Study Questions

1. In what ways did Jesus suffer humiliation, and why did He permit them?

2. The term *Puritan* was originally meant as an insult. How should we respond to the humiliation of name-calling?

3. Cotton Mather had very large, albeit false, accusations against him, which would have been humiliating to endure. Why do our enemies often try to humiliate us through lies and slander?

4. Jonathan Edwards, despite his theological brilliance, was not exempt from humiliations. How does he teach us today to wait and hope on the Lord through suffering?

5. How have you dealt with humiliation in the past? How can you better respond to it in the future?

Chapter 5

Passionately Living for Christ under Persecution

"Et tu, Brute?"

Certain phrases or scenes stick with us from books and movies. These words—"Et tu, Brute?"—have long stuck with me since first reading them some years ago. It's a Latin phrase that may be loosely translated as, "Even you, Brutus?" and it is famously spoken within William Shakespeare's *Julius Caesar* by the titular character during his assassination when he looks and notices his friend Marcus Junius Brutus.

History is uncertain about what Julius Caesar *actually* said as his last words. Some, like the Roman historian Suetonius, claim that he had said, "You too, child?" while others claim he remained silent. But the words of the play have rung throughout the centuries and have taken on a life of their own. "Et tu, Brute?" has come to symbolize unexpected betrayal by close friends and allies.

The drama in Shakespeare's scene is, of course, palpable. But the historical narrative is rather haunting as well. It was the Ides of March (March 15, 44 BC) and Caesar was meeting with the Roman senate when sixty conspirators rose against him. Wielding knives, they began their assassination attempt by stabbing Caesar. Julius attempted to fight off his assailants until he spotted Brutus, his young friend and protégé. At this point, various sources record that he stopped trying to fight altogether and merely pulled his cloak over his face so as not to see what was happening. While some say he remained quiet, others include something similar to the famous line that Shakespeare would immortalize in his play centuries later, insisting that Julius spoke a few brief words to invoke a curse on Brutus, foretelling his own brutal death, which amounted to him saying, "You too, my son, will have a taste of power."

I believe what makes this scene so hauntingly poignant and memorable is how relatable it is. There's even a great deal of similarity between this event and Judas's betrayal of Jesus. While most of us will never be conspired against and stabbed by dozens of conspirators, we can relate to the persecution that Julius underwent. We understand by experience what it is like to be conspired against. We even know, by sad experience, what it is to be betrayed by the ones we thought to be close friends and even by the ones we loved. Lord willing, we will not be physically stabbed by conspirators, but the metaphorical backs of many Christians have been plunged through with countless knives and daggers from close friends.

For the Christian, persecution is not a matter of *if*. It is simply a matter of *when*. When the persecution hits, how will the Christian respond? Is it possible, in such trying times, to truly wait and hope in our redeemer to right every wrong? The Puritans not only believed that it was possible to faithfully wait and hope on Christ in the midst of persecution; they effectively modeled it for us.

Holding to Hope through Persecution
John Calvin opened his treatise on the Lord's Supper, "The True Partaking of the Flesh and Blood of Christ," by speaking of submitting to the providential hand of God under affliction and persecution. He wrote,

> I must patiently submit to this condition which providence has assigned me—petulant, dishonest, rabid men, as if they had conspired together, must make me the special object of their virulence. Other most excellent men indeed they do not spare, assailing the living and lacerating the names of the dead; but the only cause of the more violent onset which they make on me, is, because Satan, whose slaves they are, the more useful he sees

my labours to be to the Church of Christ, stimulates them the more strongly to attack me.[1]

Calvin saw persecution as allotted to him by the providential hand of God, and therefore he had to patiently submit to it. At the same time, knowing that God was not the author of evil, he rightly understood that his persecution came from the hands of those who were themselves enslaved to Satan. In fact, the more useful he was to God's kingdom, the more he saw himself persecuted. That experience holds true not only for Calvin, not only for the Reformers, not only for the Puritans but for every saint who follows Christ. Persecution and affliction are inevitable for the one who follows Christ.

Jesus was serious when He called us to count the cost of following Him (Luke 14:28). To follow Him is to take up your cross (Matt. 16:24–26). To follow Him is to die to self and to learn to live for Him alone. It is, in short, a path filled with suffering and persecution, but leading to glory. Samuel Rutherford, who knew the path to glory was paved with necessary suffering, once wrote, "Ye will not get leave to steal quietly to heaven, in Christ's company, without a conflict and a cross.... I find crosses Christ's carved work that He marketh out for us, and that with crosses He figureth and portrayeth us to His own image, cutting away pieces of our ill and corruption. Lord cut, Lord carve, Lord wound, Lord do anything that may perfect Thy Father's image in us, and make us meet for glory."[2]

Persecution is just one of those means whereby God cuts, carves, wounds, and does what is necessary to perfect the image of God in us.

Ever since Adam and Eve ate the forbidden fruit, the righteous have been persecuted by the wicked. One need look no further than Cain's murder of Abel and it becomes immediately evident that persecution is the normative experience of all who desire to live godly lives in Jesus Christ. In fact, the apostle Paul testified to the reality of persecution when he not only wrote that he had endured great

---

1. John Calvin, "The True Partaking of the Flesh and Blood of Christ," in *Tracts and Letters*, trans. Henry Beveridge (Edinburgh: Banner of Truth, 2009), 2:498.
2. Rutherford, *Letters of Samuel Rutherford*, 547. See letter CCLXXXII.

persecution at the hands of sinners (2 Tim. 3:11) but then confirmed, "Yea, and all that will live godly in Christ Jesus shall suffer persecution" (2 Tim. 3:12).

I remember there was a time when, as a young Christian, I read 2 Timothy 3 and thought to myself, "I wonder what I'm doing wrong…. I'm just not being persecuted enough!" It was a foolish thought to have, and I truly need not have worried. It did not take long for the persecution to begin, especially when I first started preaching. Over the years, the persecution has varied in its intensity and severity, and it often takes different forms depending on the origin.

I have been called crazy for insisting that Jesus Christ alone is exclusively the way to heaven and that there is salvation in Him alone (John 14:6; Acts 4:12). I have been mercilessly mocked by others as being too "uptight" and "Puritan-esque" (ever a compliment if I heard one, actually) for upholding biblical sexual ethics. I have been slandered by those outside (and, sometimes, within) the church for both preaching the gospel and calling sinners to surrender to the lordship of Christ. I've heard silly taunts like "Bible-thumper," and more serious threats like, "I will find where you and your family live." I've lost friends, been ignored by family, and screamed at for my faith in Christ.

Honestly, the persecution I've suffered hasn't been the worst a Christian has ever experienced, nor is it peculiar to my own life. Jesus was killed on the cross by His adversaries. According to tradition, all but one of the apostles was brutally martyred for their faith in Christ. Early Christians were torn apart by lions, tied to the back of chariots and dragged through city streets, sawn asunder, boiled, flayed, crucified, and beheaded for their faith in Christ. Some of the Reformers were burned alive. Some of the Puritans were chased out of their homes, churches, and countries; some were put on trial, threatened, and imprisoned; some were executed as though they were criminals. Missionaries, throughout the whole history of Christendom, have willingly embraced persecution from those they have gone to evangelize and disciple, willingly being killed (and sometimes eaten!) by those same souls they were witnessing to. And that's just to name a few; volumes would fail to tell of the stories of these persecuted saints.

The point, however, is clear. Whether you sit in the pew or stand behind the pulpit, if you are faithful to Christ, you will be persecuted. That's the bottom line. There are no *if*s involved. You *will* be persecuted. It is not some strange thing to suffer persecution for being a follower of Christ, but normative. I cannot help but be reminded of the story of John Bunyan.

Bunyan came from a lowly family. He occupied the poor position of tinker. If ever there was a miserable wretch to walk the earth, it was Bunyan—he would even go on to title his own autobiography *Grace Abounding to the Chief of Sinners*. But after his conversion, there was an incredible transformation that took place in the tinker's life: while he never really stopped being poor during his lifetime (even his significant fame brought about by many book sales was not enough to lift his family completely from poverty), he did stop his wicked, conniving, and rotten ways.

One might expect that his neighbors would have been profoundly impacted by the change in the tinker. Admittedly, they were amazed by the moral changes that had taken place. The problem was that his neighbors made a very large deal about his morality *before* he was actually converted. Bunyan explains the problem in his own words:

> But, I say, my neighbours were amazed at this my great conversion, from prodigious profaneness, to something like a moral life; and truly, so they well might; for this my conversion was as great, as for Tom of Bethlehem to become a sober man. Now therefore they began to praise, to commend, and to speak well of me, both to my face, and behind my back. Now I was, as they said, become godly; now I was become a right honest man. But oh! when I understood these were their words and opinions of me, it pleased me mighty well. For, though as yet I was nothing but a poor painted hypocrite, yet, I loved to be talked of as one that was truly godly. I was proud of my godliness, and indeed,

> I did all I did, either to be seen of, or to be well spoken of, by men: and thus I continued for about a twelvemonth, or more.[3]

Amazed by his newfound morality, they praised him for his good deeds and failed to point him to the Lord. But when he was *finally* and truly converted, would the people praise him then?

As the Lord would have it, the answer was a resounding no. Rather than praise him, they ought to have praised the Lord, but they would not even do this. Instead, they sought to knock him down as many pegs as they could and to call into question his right to preach the gospel. In fact, it was only a few years into his public ministry that he found himself being arrested for preaching the gospel.

Bunyan rightly deduced that the manner in which he handled the persecution would either glorify God or hurt his own ability to continue ministering to others. He also concluded that though God was able to use the persecution for the good of His kingdom, it was delivered unto him by the hand of Satan: "Now as Satan laboured by reproaches and slanders, to make me vile among my countrymen; that, if possible, my preaching might be made of none effect; so there was added hereto, a long and tedious imprisonment, that thereby I might be frightened from my service for Christ, and the world terrified, and made afraid to hear me preach."[4]

So it was that one day, before the tinker was about to preach, he found himself being arrested:

> Having made profession of the glorious gospel of Christ a long time, and preached the same about five years, I was apprehended at a meeting of good people in the country (among whom, had they let me alone, I should have preached that day, but they took me away from amongst them), and had me before a justice; who, after I had offered security for my appearing at the next sessions, yet committed me, because my sureties

---

3. John Bunyan, *Grace Abounding to the Chief of Sinners*, in *The Works of John Bunyan* (Edinburgh: Banner of Truth, 1991), 1:32.
4. Bunyan, *Grace Abounding*, 1:317.

would not consent to be bound that I should preach no more to the people.[5]

As Satan has often done throughout the history of Christendom, he attacked one of God's ministers in such a way that he likely anticipated Bunyan would stop preaching altogether. In fact, it seems that our enemies persecute us with the intention that we stop serving God publicly. With threatenings, revilings, false accusations, rumors, and violence, the enemies of Christ have long lifted both their voices and fists against the people of God. But such persecutions must never be permitted to stop our service to the Lord. When our enemies threaten to do their worst and demand we stop speaking of Jesus, worshiping Jesus, or serving Jesus, we must take our stand with the apostles and boldly proclaim, "We ought to obey God rather than men" (Acts 5:29). At such times as these, the Lord will refresh and quicken us to remain steadfast in the work he has called us to, though the road be paved with persecution.

Bunyan was freed from prison eventually. But during that period of extreme persecution, he did not waver in service to the Lord. He wrote *The Pilgrim's Progress* while imprisoned, along with some other works. And, once he was freed, he went immediately back to preaching. For him, waiting on the Lord and hoping in Him taught him that persecution was a time to grow in grace rather than anguish.

Blessed Are They Who Are Persecuted for Christ's Sake
Bunyan models for us the way in which the Puritans suffered through things like persecution with continual hope. The question then is, What do the Puritans teach us to do with persecution? If it is truly normative, how are we to handle and deal with it? How are we to wait and hope in Christ while suffering through it? Bunyan learned the answer while in prison:

> I never knew what it was for God to stand by me at all turns, and at every offer of Satan to afflict me, etc., as I have found Him since I came in hither: for look how fears have presented

---

5. Bunyan, *Grace Abounding*, 1:318.

themselves, so have supports and encouragements; yea, when I have started, even as it were, at nothing else but my shadow, yet God, as being very tender of me, hath not suffered me to be molested, but would with one scripture or another, strengthen me against all; insomuch that I have often said, *were it lawful, I could pray for greater trouble, for the greater comfort's sake.*[6]

Bunyan's comforts from the Lord, in the midst of persecution, came through the Scriptures. We do well to learn from him and alongside him.

Let us then turn our attention to the words of Jesus and begin by first recognizing the blessing of persecution. In the Sermon on the Mount, Jesus touched on this idea of persecution as blessing in His eighth beatitude. In Matthew 5:10–12, He said this: "Blessed are they which are persecuted for righteousness' sake: for theirs is the kingdom of heaven. Blessed are ye, when men shall revile you, and persecute you, and shall say all manner of evil against you falsely, for my sake. Rejoice, and be exceeding glad: for great is your reward in heaven: for so persecuted they the prophets which were before you."

First, to understand the eighth beatitude and Jesus's commentary on it, we have to understand that the blessing promised to us does not exist because of the trial or suffering but is promised to the saint who is going through the suffering or the trial. Believe me, I know there is very little blessing felt when we are persecuted, and we are slandered and reviled, and all manner of cruel things are said of us. But the blessing is not the persecution; it's what follows.

What we have in this eighth beatitude is the dynamic of the "already/not yet." We who have been saved by Jesus do not yet have the full sense of the blessing that is ours in Christ, but we do have some of that blessing. The fullest sense of it will be experienced when Jesus makes all things new on the earth, when He both judges evil and rewards us as His saints. When we are with the Lord forevermore, we will truly be comforted, every tear will be wiped from our

---

6. Bunyan, *Grace Abounding*, 1:323.

eyes, and we will have the fullest sense of joy and happiness in being joined together to Jesus forevermore.

But there is a sense in which we have some of this blessing now. The word Jesus uses in the Greek is μακάριος (*makarios*), and it means to be blessed in the sense of receiving God's favor. It means to be most fortunate, most in a position of favor. It means to be made most happy precisely because we know we have God's favor. It is not that God promises we will never have trials; on the contrary, "all that will live godly in Christ Jesus shall suffer persecution" (2 Tim. 3:12). The promise is that God will see us through the trials and the suffering and that we will experience the blessing of His smiling face and tender care in the final analysis.

The blessing, then, is *not* the persecution but rather our reception into the kingdom of heaven. The persecution merely serves as a tool whereby we can, as Rutherford wrote, be cut and carved until God's image is perfected within us. The blessing is that God brings us into His very own kingdom. The blessing is that God's kingdom is now ours, and we will one day rule alongside Christ. Persecution makes us ready for such a time as this.

Dear Christian, are you reviled? Persecuted? Do others utter falsehoods and evil against you because of your allegiance to Christ? Then be of good cheer! They persecuted Jesus. They persecuted the prophets. They persecuted every Christian who came before you. You are in good company! Just as each of them received a great reward in heaven, so too will we.

Beloved, God will vindicate us. He will vindicate me. He will vindicate you. Injustices will not go unpunished. This is why, at the end of the day, despite the rumors that swirl around us and the false accusations that are made against us daily, we must not return evil for evil. We must refuse to speak ill of others, even when they persecute. Vengeance is the Lord's, not our own (Ps. 94:1). Let us simply labor for peace and not return evil for evil. We are, after all, the citizens of heaven and sons of the living God!

Let our enemies say what they will. Let them have at it and

persecute us. It was Charles Spurgeon, preaching on how David was persecuted by his wife Michal, who famously said,

> Brother, if any man thinks ill of you, do not be angry with him. For you are worse than he thinks you to be. If he charges you falsely on some point, yet be satisfied, for if he knew you better he might change the accusation and you would be no gainer by the correction. If you have your moral portrait painted and it is ugly, be satisfied. For it only needs a few blacker touches and it would be still nearer the truth.[7]

Spurgeon, of course, was right. We are far worse than we realize. So let us repent of our wickedness and, simultaneously, embrace persecution as a gift from God whereby we learn humility and dependence on Him. Let us be satisfied in God and recant the anger we would otherwise feel toward our persecutors.

At the same time, let us remember that God knows the truth. He will vindicate me. He will vindicate you. The arms of our enemies are too short to box with God. Just as surely as His kingdom will come and His will *will* be done, we shall be vindicated. We shall enjoy citizenship in the heavenly kingdom and inherit the earth. Despite persecution, we are most blessed indeed, for the kingdom of heaven is ours, and we are being molded and made fit to enter this kingdom.

"You Too, Judas?": Betrayal in the House of God
I said at the start of this chapter that Shakespeare's scene of Julius Caesar's betrayal has haunted me since first discovering it. It's not the only scene of betrayal from a book or a movie that has stuck with me.

Growing up as a kid in Long Island, I remember often going to a large public library where it seemed I could find just about any book imaginable. If my parents would have permitted it, I would have spent countless hours wandering the aisles of bloated shelves, skimming pages, and reading the books that struck my fancy.

---

7. Charles Spurgeon, "David Dancing before the Ark Because of His Election," Christian Classics Ethereal Library, accessed December 2, 2023, https://www.ccel.org/ccel/spurgeon/sermons34.xxix.html.

It was around 2005 when C. S. Lewis's *The Lion, the Witch, and the Wardrobe* was turned into a big movie and the library was advertising *The Chronicles of Narnia* series of books with big displays and posters. So, I picked the first one up, checked it out, and was so captivated by it, I quickly finished it. I loved the idea of a magical wardrobe that transported children into a land called Narnia. I loved the Pevensie children and was terribly dismayed when one—Edmund—betrayed his family to the White Witch for thirty pieces of Turkish delight (the allusion to Judas betraying Jesus for thirty pieces of silver was intentional).

While Edmund was ultimately redeemed by the end of the tale, it was shocking for me to realize that even family might betray us. It was truly a compelling story for a child, but it also taught me a valuable lesson: Sometimes the worst of persecution can come from those we thought were our closest allies.

It happened to David in the Bible. King Saul, whom David served faithfully, fought for, and played music for, attempted to kill him on multiple occasions. Reflecting on this (and simultaneously prophesying about the Messiah's betrayal by one of His closest friends), David wrote in Psalm 55:12-14, "For it was not an enemy that reproached me; then I could have borne it: neither was it he that hated me that did magnify himself against me; then I would have hid myself from him: but it was thou, a man mine equal, my guide, and mine acquaintance. We took sweet counsel together, and walked unto the house of God in company."

There is something tragically lamentable about betrayal by a close friend. Persecution from someone we have never been close to or simply do not know is hard, but it probably won't make us lose sleep. But being betrayed by a friend, family member, or close acquaintance and then being persecuted by them? That's more than difficult; it is, at times, almost unbearable.

Jesus, of course, knew this sort of betrayal and persecution firsthand. We are reminded that Judas Iscariot was one of the Twelve called specifically by Jesus to serve alongside Him during His earthly ministry. He handled the money and probably had a good reputation among others. After all, when Judas leaves the dinner table to go and betray Jesus, the others think he is merely going to give money to the poor, completely in the dark that he was stealing money!

Regardless, we have no reason to believe that Jesus was not close to Judas. He appears to have been close with all members of the Twelve. And that, in part, makes Luke 22:47–48 so shocking when it recounts the betrayal: "And while he yet spake, behold a multitude, and he that was called Judas, one of the twelve, went before them, and drew near unto Jesus to kiss him. But Jesus said unto him, Judas, betrayest thou the Son of man with a kiss?"

Sadly, I have been in scenarios similar to this one. I have been through church splits where pastors whom I loved and trusted suddenly bore their fangs and acted as wolves are keen to do and scattered the flock.

I have had ideas stolen by those I truly thought were praying for my success.

I have been cast aside by those I gave my all to; those whom I was willing to die for plunged their knives into my back when I least suspected.

I have been abandoned by those who promised to stick with me, right at those moments I needed them most.

I have been lied about by those I counted as allies, gossiped about by those I thought I could trust, ridiculed and betrayed by those whom I loved.

This sort of betrayal and persecution is always exponentially worse than when we are persecuted by those we have had no relationship with. But the good news is this: Jesus can both relate and comfort us through these trials. As the author of Hebrews wrote,

> Seeing then that we have a great high priest, that is passed into the heavens, Jesus the Son of God, let us hold fast our profession. For we have not an high priest which cannot be touched with the feeling of our infirmities; but was in all points tempted like as we are, yet without sin. Let us therefore come boldly unto the throne of grace, that we may obtain mercy, and find grace to help in time of need. (4:14–16)

When you find yourself surrounded in darkness, at the bottom of some dank, old cellar of the soul, do not forget Christ. He will not only protect you through the persecution and betrayal but will satisfy the deepest longings and cravings of your soul. As Samuel Rutherford wrote, there is rich wine to be discovered in God's cellars:

> But for you, hing on; your feast is not far off; ye shall be filled ere ye go. There is as much in our Lord's pantry as will satisfy all His bairns, and as much wine in His cellar as will quench all their thirst. Hunger on, for there is meat in hunger for Christ. Never go from Him, but fash Him (who yet is pleased with the importunity of hungry souls) with a dish-full of hungry desires till He fill you; and if He delay, yet come not ye away, albeit ye should fall aswoon at His feet.[8]

A Cautioning Word

Now, for a word of warning: the last thing I want is for someone reading this chapter to walk away thinking they need to go find new ways to suffer persecution. During the Middle Ages, many Christians adopted monastic and ascetic lifestyles by traveling into the desert and cutting themselves off from society, thinking such a life of denial would make them more spiritual and holy. Please do not misread this chapter as suggesting that persecution is a defining mark of great spirituality and holiness. Persecution *will* come for the godly, but it does not need to be sought out, nor is it the litmus test whereby we determine whether we are saved.

However, because persecution has been normative, it can be quite strange *not* to suffer persecution. Yet there is still room to wait and hope on Christ even in these periods and areas of relative peace and comfort. We can and should do certain things as Christians, and within our churches, even when there is no serious persecution occurring. Missiologist Robin Hadaway explains it this way:

> Persecution certainly purifies the church and is a positive factor in church growth. The Christians I know in limited-access

---

8. Rutherford, *Letters of Samuel Rutherford*, 492. See letter CCXLIX.

countries, however, pray persecution will stop in their nation, although they acknowledge it eliminates most insincere believers. The church in the nonpersecuted world should focus on meaningful small groups, including, but not exclusively, house and cell churches, to recapture something of the esprit de corps and vitality of the early church. Although a weekly dinner might be a stretch in the modern world, pastors and church leaders should attempt to imitate the intimate fellowship of the early church that such practices encourage.[9]

In short, don't seek out persecution! Nothing would be more foolish than this. If you're desiring to live a godly life in Christ Jesus, it *will* come. But we ought to do our best, whether in times of peace or tumult, to draw close to our local church bodies. The communion of the saints is an essential part of your union and walk with Christ. You need the saints if you have any hope of enduring persecution with hope.

Don't run from persecution either, though. This, too, would be a mistake. To flee persecution would be to cut yourself off from the world, and Christ calls us to stand indomitable and bold before persecution. He calls us to wait on Him and hope in Him even when the whole world has seemingly turned against us. Like Saint Athanasius being told the whole world was against him for upholding the doctrine of the Trinity, we must look at a world warring against us and courageously answer, "If the whole world is against me, then I am against the whole world." Such apparently insurmountable odds can and will be surmounted by the grace of God. Again, as Rutherford wrote, "If your Lord call you to suffering, be not dismayed; there shall be a new allowance of the King for you when you come to it. One of the softest pillows Christ hath is laid under His witnesses' head, though often they must set down their bare feet among thorns."[10]

As we meditate on the theme of enduring persecution for Christ's sake, let us also reflect on this prayer from Arthur Bennett:

---

9. Robin A. Hadaway, *A Survey of World Missions* (Nashville, Tenn.: B&H Publishing, 2020), 91.

10. Rutherford, *Letters of Samuel Rutherford*, 309. See letter CLXV.

If thou hast appointed storms of tribulation,
   thou wilt be with me in them;
If I have to pass through tempests of persecution
   and temptation,
I shall not drown;
If I am to die,
I shall see thy face the sooner;
If a painful end is to be my lot,
   grant me grace that my faith fail not;
If I am to be cast aside from the service I love,
I can make no stipulation;
Only glorify thyself in me whether in comfort or trial,
   as a chosen vessel meet always for thy use.[11] Amen.

Study Questions

1. From Jesus to Paul to countless others, persecution has been a normal experience for Christians. Why are Christians persecuted in this world?

2. "Yea, and all that will live godly in Christ Jesus shall suffer persecution" (2 Tim. 3:12). Persecution is a matter of *when*, not *if*. Why does God permit persecution in the lives of His saints?

3. John Bunyan was not only persecuted but imprisoned for an extended period because of his faith. What do we learn from him and his response?

4. "Et tu, Brute?" has immortalized unexpected betrayal. Have you ever been betrayed? How did you react? How does the Bible teach us to respond?

5. We need not seek persecution as Christians; with time, it will come. But what promises of Scripture provide us with the strength needed to wait and hope when persecution comes?

---

11. Arthur Bennett, "A Prayer for Year's End," in *The Valley of Vision* (Edinburgh: Banner of Truth, 1975), 111.

Chapter 6

Living as Outcasts, Vagabonds, and Pilgrims with Joy

August 24, 1662, marked both the annual celebration of St. Bartholomew's Day and the day on which over twenty-five hundred Puritan ministers were ejected from their pulpits for refusing to comply with the Act of Uniformity, which demanded all ministers of the Church of England adhere to the 1662 Book of Common Prayer.

These faithful ministers were literally cast out from their pulpits, churches, and even homes. The ejected men included Thomas Manton, John Flavel, Richard Baxter, Thomas Brooks, and many, many others.

This may make the Puritans sound as though they were unreasonable or, at the very least, the cause of their own problems. Why could they not simply comply with these orders from King Charles II? But this was no mere childish tantrum; for the Puritans, it was essential that they be permitted to pray extemporaneously while also distancing themselves far from the written liturgies of Rome. They insisted on the right to worship God as He had commanded in His Word, while also not being held to any standards that He Himself has not explicitly commanded.

Some of the Puritans attempted to reason with the king and Parliament. Richard Baxter, in particular, worked to create and compile a thoroughly Reformed liturgy, which would have then taken the place of the 1662 Book of Common Prayer. But it was not to be. As Baxter later recorded,

I have reason to think that the generality of the bishops and doctors present, never knew what we offered them in the reformed liturgy, nor in this reply, nor in any of our papers, save those few which we read openly to them; for they were put up and carried away; and, I conjecture, scarce any but the writers of their confutations would be at the labor of reading them over.... So that, it seems, before they knew what was in them, they resolved to reject our papers, right or wrong, and to deliver them up to their contradictors.[1]

Those who had rejected the Puritans were dead set against them. Even Baxter's attempts to appease the authorities with a distinctly Reformed written liturgy was not enough. The Puritans would be ejected, and there was truly nothing they could do to prevent this travesty from happening. And yet the Puritans continued to preach and write some of their finest sermons during this time.

Can you relate? Surely you can. At the very least, you must become familiar with stories like that of the Great Ejection, for such stories are common to the Christian experience.

Stop me if you've heard this one before.[2]

Cast Out by the World, but Never Cast Out by Christ

He was a new Christian. While he certainly did not understand all the theological or doctrinal truths that a more seasoned Christian would learn over time, he knew that Jesus had saved his soul and blessed him. A miracle of momentous proportions had occurred in his life. Though he was born blind, now he could see. Though he was lost, now he was found. For all of this, he had Jesus to thank. His main desire now was to know Christ and make Him known to the world. But as he went forth to share with others the good news of what Jesus had done for him, something shocking happened: the people cast him out of their fellowship.

---

1. Recorded in William Orme, *Life and Times of the Rev. Richard Baxter with a Critical Examination of His Writings* (Boston: Crocker and Brewster, 1831), 1:186.

2. The following example is taken and adapted from my article, "Cast Out by the World; Never Cast Out by Christ," G3 Ministries, July 15, 2022, https://g3min.org/cast-out-by-the-world-never-cast-out-by-christ/.

If this story sounds familiar, that's because it's the story of the man who had been born blind, whom Jesus healed in John 9 and was later cast out of the synagogue for professing that Jesus had healed him. It is also familiar to us because, without fail, every Christian either has experienced a moment like this or, unfortunately, will. This is not mere pessimism but the promise of our Lord Himself: "And ye shall be hated of all men for my name's sake: but he that endureth to the end shall be saved.... Then shall they deliver you up to be afflicted, and shall kill you: and ye shall be hated of all nations for my name's sake" (Matt. 10:22; 24:9).

The Great Ejection attests to these truths. As a pastor, even I can attest to this reality. We're often surrounded by wolves in sheep's clothing, just waiting to unzip their costume so they can step out and bare their fangs. We're surrounded by a hostile culture that hates all that is holy, good, and true. Is it any surprise that our allegiance to Christ as Lord leads to the world's hatred of us?

What is a Christian to do when these trials and hardships come? Note carefully that it is not a question of what should be done *if* the Christian suffers rejection and persecution from the world but rather what should be done *when* the Christian suffers these things. The Puritans could attest to the inevitability of being rejected by the world. Yet, for both newer Christians and seasoned Christians alike, for those infants in the faith and those who are mature, this remains an important question: What should the Christian do when the world rejects them? Thankfully, the Word of God both instructs and encourages on this front in many places, especially in John 9.

Making God's Grace Known Is Worth the Persecution
When we first meet the man born blind of John 9, he is begging outside the synagogue. He is not only blind but is destitute and dead in sin. But Jesus looks on him and shows this poor man mercy and grace. He heals his eyes and saves his soul (John 9:1–7). This an amazing act of mercy and grace, and the man cannot help but go and share the good news with others. We who have experienced the grace of God must do the same.

The now seeing man, however, is not met with the cheerful joy and acceptance he may have expected. Instead, the Pharisees refuse to believe him and they threaten his parents, tell him to deny Jesus, and, finally, cast him out of the synagogue for professing Jesus (John 9:8–34).

Despite their threatening him, the man could not help but give a verbal confession of the truth. In John 9:25, he confessed, "Whether he be a sinner or no, I know not: one thing I know, that, whereas I was blind, now I see." What an incredible testimony! Then, in verses 30–33, the man explains how Jesus is the perfect, sinless, heaven-sent, virgin-born Son of the living God.

Verse 34 is the kicker, though. He's been healed and saved by Jesus, and his life has changed. Things are really looking up. But his confession of Jesus leads directly to his being cast out of the synagogue when the religious leaders look at him and say, "'Thou wast altogether born in sins, and dost thou teach us?' And they cast him out."

Today, Christians must expect and endure rejection, speaking the truth all the same as pilgrims and outcasts. The apostle Paul promised persecution for godliness in 2 Timothy 3:12 when he wrote, "Yea, and all that will live godly in Christ Jesus shall suffer persecution." Frankly, the Christian who never experiences any sort of persecution from the world should be concerned! For godliness may be great gain with the Lord but will inevitably lead to clashes within the culture. Each Christian is effectively an outcast pilgrim whose home is not in the world but rather in the celestial city, where our citizenship is with Christ (Phil. 3:20).

We Must Find Our Comfort in Christ, Who Sees and Knows All
One of the great encouragements afforded to the Christian is that Jesus sees, hears, and knows all. No sooner is the man cast out of the synagogue than Jesus makes His way over to comfort him. "Jesus heard that they had cast him out; and when he had found him, he said unto him, Dost thou believe on the Son of God?" (John 9:35). We serve a Savior who does not delay in tenderly caring for His sheep. He is in no danger of missing any injustice done to us in our lives, nor is

He capable of turning a blind eye to what occurs. He not only invites us to rest in Him by casting our cares and burdens on Him (Matt. 11:28–30; 1 Peter 5:7) but He immediately comes to our aid when we need Him most. As the author of Hebrews encourages us,

> For ye have need of patience, that, after ye have done the will of God, ye might receive the promise. For yet a little while, and he that shall come will come, and will not tarry. Now the just shall live by faith: but if any man draw back, my soul shall have no pleasure in him. But we are not of them who draw back unto perdition; but of them that believe to the saving of the soul. (10:36–39)

John Bunyan knew the trials of rejection, being cast out from the pulpit and even arrested for the faith. Yet he also knew the great comfort of the assurance that Christ will *never* cast out His elect, no matter what the world may decide to do in turn. In his wonderful *Come and Welcome to Jesus Christ*, Bunyan assures his readers of Christ's promise, "I will in no wise cast out" (John 6:37):

> For had there not been a proneness in us to "fear casting out," Christ needed not to have, as it were, waylaid our fear, as he doth by this great and strange expression, "In no wise"; "And him that cometh to me I will in no wise cast out." There needed not, as I may say, such a promise to be invented by the wisdom of heaven, and worded at such a rate, as it were on purpose to dash in pieces at one blow all the objections of coming sinners, if they were not prone to admit of such objections, to the discouraging of their own souls. For this word, "in no wise," cutteth the throat of all objections; and it was dropped by the Lord Jesus for that very end; and to help the faith that is mixed with unbelief. And it is, as it were, the sum of all promises; neither can any objection be made upon the unworthiness that thou findest in thee, that this promise will not assoil.
>
> But I am a great sinner, sayest thou. "I will in no wise cast out," says Christ. But I am an old sinner, sayest thou. "I will in no wise cast out," says Christ. But I am a hard-hearted sinner, sayest thou. "I will in nowise cast out," says Christ. But I am a backsliding sinner, sayest thou. "I will in no wise cast out," says

Christ. But I have served Satan all my days, sayest thou. "I will in no wise cast out," says Christ. But I have sinned against light, sayest thou. "I will in no wise cast out," says Christ. But I have sinned against mercy, sayest thou. "I will in no wise cast out," says Christ. But I have no good thing to bring with me, sayest thou. "I will in no wise cast out," says Christ.

Thus I might go on to the end of things, and show you, that still this promise was provided to answer all objections, and doth answer them.[3]

We, like Bunyan, must find comfort in the sovereign hands of our faithful God. We must also know that as surely as our comfort is in Christ, so too is our vindication (Ps. 94:1; Rom. 12:19). Not only will He not leave or forsake us (Heb. 13:5); He will not allow injustices and sins against us to go unpunished, for "neither is there any creature that is not manifest in his sight: but all things are naked and opened unto the eyes of him with whom we have to do" (Heb. 4:13).

We Must Remember That Though the World Cast Us Out, We Will Never Be Cast Out by Christ

John 9:34 is juxtaposed against John 6:37. Of the Pharisees, we read, "And they cast him out." But of Christ we read, "All that the Father giveth me shall come to me; and him that cometh to me I will in no wise cast out."

What Christ offers the sinner is an eternal communion. What the world offers is only temporal and fleeting. Should the world cast us out for our faith in Christ, we have lost nothing. Let the world do its worst. Gladly accept this world's injustices, discriminations, persecutions, vitriol, and hatred, for then we know that we have been counted worthy to share in the sufferings and afflictions of Jesus (Acts 5:41; Col. 1:24; 1 Peter 5:9–10). If we have Christ, we can have confidence and boldness in our declarations of truth.

---

3. John Bunyan, *Come and Welcome to Jesus Christ: A Plain and Profitable Discourse on John 6:37*, in *The Works of John Bunyan* (Edinburgh: Banner of Truth, 1991), 1:279–80.

Live joyfully as outcast pilgrims and vagabonds. Find both your comfort and courage in Christ. We do not need cowardly Christians today, afraid of the world's rejection, but courageous Christians who know their Savior and hope in His promises.

Furthermore, if we have Jesus, we can rest in His strong hands, knowing not only that He will never cast us out but that nothing can pluck us from His hands (John 10:28–30; Rom. 8:31–39). We may be cast out by the world, but Christ will never cast out His own.

The Dangers of Earthly Mindedness
Why were the Puritans able to endure such great rejection from sinful men? Why was the man of John 9 able to find joy in Christ even though he was effectively rejected by whatever friends and family he knew? Ultimately, it was because these saints were heavenly minded rather than earthly minded.

Jeremiah Burroughs wrote an entire book on the dangers of earthly mindedness. He explained,

> Earthly things are those that are on the earth, whatever they are, the beauty, the glory, and pageantry of the earth; the profits that are earthly, the pleasures and honors of the world; who mind any things inordinately that are sublunary accommodations. But we carry and behave ourselves as free citizens of the city of Heaven, for so the words in the original are, if we should thus read them, "Our city, where we are citizens and where we have rights, is heaven."[4]

The Christian who knows their citizenship is in heaven should have no desire for the things of this earth. Yet one of the sorest vexations for the one who is earthly minded is an overwhelming desire to be loved, accepted, and applauded by the world. This, of course, flies in the face of Scripture's clear warning: "Ye adulterers and adulteresses, know ye not that the friendship of the world is enmity with God? whosoever therefore will be a friend of the world is the enemy

---

4. Jeremiah Burroughs, *A Treatise on Earthly-Mindedness* (1649; repr., Grand Rapids: Soli Deo Gloria, 2022), 4.

of God" (James 4:4). Those who desire this world's love will often nearly kill themselves in trying to get it.

Worse yet, though, is the pitiful situation that befalls the one who actually gets what they want from this world. When the earthly minded man gets what he wants, he is both distanced from God and woefully incapable of dealing with the rejection of the world. What is he to do when the world hates him? He can do little more than lament and weep, for he has lost the only thing he ever truly cared for.

If Christians will learn how to wait and hope, even through rejection, then we must pay careful attention to the teaching of Jeremiah Burroughs. He warns, "If riches increase, do not set your hearts upon them. If friends increase, do not set your hearts upon them, but trust in the living God. Let it be the living God whom you rest on for all outward things in the world."[5] This is a truth we must never lose sight of. Our satisfaction comes *not* from the things of this world. Earthly riches cannot eternally satisfy. Friends cannot eternally satisfy. Only Christ can eternally satisfy. This is why Jesus encourages His children to "lay not up for yourselves treasures upon earth, where moth and rust doth corrupt, and where thieves break through and steal: but lay up for yourselves treasures in heaven, where neither moth nor rust doth corrupt, and where thieves do not break through nor steal: for where your treasure is, there will your heart be also" (Matt. 6:19–21).

If you set your eyes on earthly riches, or the vanity of popularity, fame, and so-called worldly success, then your heart will be set on the earth. You will never be able to faithfully endure the trials of rejection.

But if your treasure is in heaven, then your heart will be there as well. We must see that Jesus Himself is our heavenly treasure, and indeed no moth or rust can corrupt Him; no thief can break in and steal Him; nothing can remove or take this treasure from us. We may live on this earth as vagabond pilgrims and outcasts, but if we have Christ, we have enough. Let us be content in Christ, who alone is our true eternal treasure, and let us set our heart's gaze and affections on

---

5. Burroughs, *Treatise on Earthly-Mindedness*, 60.

Him, for then we will be heavenly minded and much more able to endure rejection.

The Great Things Accomplished by Outcasts for God

Let the reader understand that despite the world's animosity, when a Christian is heavenly minded, great things for God may still be accomplished. Consider, for example, the story of George Whitefield (who was technically a Calvinistic Methodist, but I include him here as one who followed in the spirit of the Puritans). Whitefield was despised by the world, but he even had friends and allies oppose his preaching of the gospel and the doctrines of grace.

Many times, it appeared as though Whitefield stood utterly alone. Though they would eventually reconcile, the Wesley brothers—especially John Wesley—stood against Whitefield after he embraced Calvinism. Though they were formerly close friends and allies, doctrine divided them. At the same time, Whitefield hardly seemed able to go anywhere to preach the gospel without meeting some adversity or another.

Yet it is debatable if any other man had quite as great an impact on the Great Awakening of the eighteenth century as he did. He preached all over Europe *and* America and made acquaintances with figures such as Jonathan Edwards and even Benjamin Franklin. Despite the disdain of many toward him, his gospel impact was undeniable.

Consider the story of the revival at Moorfields. Whitefield, in a letter dated May 11, 1742, recorded how a revival broke out at Moorfields, London. It was the Easter season, and thousands were gathered, but not for Whitefield. For some years, stages and booths were constructed at Moorfields for the express purpose of putting on plays and puppet shows. But on this one day (which some have suggested was likely April 19, 1742),[6] Whitefield records how he seized an opportunity to preach the gospel. Though it is a lengthy account,

---

6. Arnold Dallimore, *George Whitefield: The Life and Times of the Great Evangelist of the 18th Century Revival* (Edinburgh: Banner of Truth, 1980), 2:115. Dallimore's phenomenal biography first alerted me to the account I have recorded here, which he also recorded in his work on Whitefield.

I record the whole event here so that the reader may understand the paradoxical nature of how we may be simultaneously cast out by the world while experiencing the great riches and rewards of following Christ:

> Perhaps there were about ten thousand in waiting, not for me, but for Satan's instruments to amuse them.—Glad was I to find, that I had for once as it were got the start of the devil.
>
> I mounted my field pulpit, almost all flocked immediately around it. I preached on these words, "As Moses lifted up the serpent in the wilderness, so shall the son of man be lifted up, &c." They gazed, they listened, they wept; and I believe that many felt themselves stung with deep conviction for their past sins. All was hushed and solemn.
>
> Being thus encouraged, I ventured out again at noon; but what a scene! The fields, the whole fields seemed, in a bad sense of the word, all white, ready not for the Redeemer's, but Beelzebub's harvest. All his agents were in full motion, drummers, trumpeters, merry andrews, masters of puppet shows, exhibiters of wild beasts, players, &c. &c. all busy in entertaining their respective auditories. I suppose there could not be less than twenty or thirty thousand people.
>
> My pulpit was fixed on the opposite side, and immediately, to their great mortification, they found the number of their attendants sadly lessened. Judging that like saint Paul, I should now be called as it were to fight with beasts at Ephesus, I preached from these words: "Great is Diana of the Ephesians." You may easily guess, that there was some noise among the craftsmen, and that I was honoured with having a few stones, dirt, rotten eggs, and pieces of dead cats thrown at me, whilst engaged in calling them from their favourite but lying vanities. My soul was indeed among lions; but far the greatest part of my congregation, which was very large, seemed for a while to be turned into lambs. This encouraged me to give notice, that I would preach again at six o'clock in the evening.
>
> I came, I saw, but what—thousands and thousands more than before if possible, still more deeply engaged in their unhappy diversions; but some thousands amongst them waiting as earnestly to hear the gospel.

This Satan could not brook. One of his choicest servants was exhibiting, trumpeting on a large stage; but as soon as the people saw me in my black robes and my pulpit, I think all to a man left him and ran to me. For a while I was enabled to lift up my voice like a trumpet, and many heard the joyful sound.

God's people kept praying, and the enemy's agents made a kind of a roaring at some distance from our camp. At length they approached nearer, and the merry andrew (attended by others, who complained that they had taken many pounds less that day on account of my preaching) got upon a man's shoulders, and advancing near the pulpit attempted to slash me with a long heavy whip several times, but always with the violence of his motion tumbled down.

Soon afterwards, they got a recruiting serjeant with his drum, &c. to pass through the congregation. I gave the word of command, and ordered that way might be made for the king's officer. The ranks opened, while all march'd quietly through, and then closed again.

Finding those efforts to fail, a large body quite on the opposite side assembled together, and having got a large pole for their standard, advanced towards us with steady and formidable steps, till they came very near the skirts of our hearing, praying, and almost undaunted congregation. I saw, gave warning, and prayed to the captain of our salvation for present support and deliverance. He heard and answered; for just as they approached us with looks full of resentment, I know not by what accident, they quarrelled among themselves, threw down their staff and went their way, leaving however many of their company behind, who before we had done, I trust were brought over to join the besieged party.

I think I continued in praying preaching, and singing, (for the noise was too great at times to preach) about three hours.[7]

"I was honoured with having a few stones, dirt, rotten eggs, and pieces of dead cats thrown at me." Can you imagine the horror of such a situation? There stood the great preacher being pelted with the trash, debris, and dead things of a hateful mob. As though the

---

7. George Whitefield, *Works* (London: Edward and Charles Dilly, in the Poultry; and Messrs. Kincaid and Bell, at Edinburgh, 1771), 1:384–86.

stones, dirt, and eggs weren't enough, the mob actually threw pieces of *dead cats.*

If that doesn't describe what it is to be cast out and rejected by the world, I'm not sure what does. Whitefield was absolutely hated by the people in that crowd who wanted no part of God's Word but desired only to continue in their sin. Yet, in love, Whitefield continued to testify to the gospel of grace in Jesus Christ, earnestly praying that the same people who had troubled themselves to throw dead cats at him would be irresistibly drawn to salvation in Christ. He was not earthly minded, but heavenly minded. He knew his treasure was Christ Himself. The world could cast him out, but he knew Christ never would. All of this gave him the strength to keep pressing on for Christ.

Despite the attempts of the crowd to stop Whitefield, he continued to preach. Try as they may, with distractions, violence, and even roaring, they could not stop Whitefield because, ultimately, they could not stop God.

Waiting and Hoping as Outcasts

By way of encouragement to every saint battling the evils of this world, and by way of warning to those who oppose the Lord Jesus Christ and His people, read these words carefully. Those who oppose King Jesus, the coming of His kingdom, the building of His church, the salvation of sinners, and the accomplishment of His will, will find this one statement to be irrevocably true: *your arms are too short to box with God.*

Christ's kingdom will come, His church will be built, every last sinner promised Him by the Father will be saved, and His will *will* be done.

This is inevitable. Nothing will delay, slow, or frustrate His plans. The nations will be conquered and discipled, and the globalization of Christendom will come to pass. It may not be in our generation or even within ten generations from now, but mark this: it will happen. Just as surely as men die and, after this, undergo the judgment (Heb. 9:27), just as surely as God is unchanging (James 1:17), just as surely as Jesus is coming back (John 14:3; Acts 1:11; Rev. 1:7–8),

Christ will surely subjugate the nations through the gospel, conquer His foes, strike down His enemies with sword in mouth (Rev. 19:15), and hold up His precious saints—His bride—as a treasured crown (1 Thess. 2:19).

We need more Whitefields and Burroughses today. We need more men with that indomitable Puritan spirit who are willing to be rejected by this cruel world, if only they may have the love of Christ. We need men of virtue and valor who will not shrink in the face of evil nor stumble when the world shakes its fist at them for following Christ. We need Christians who know that, like the man cast out from the synagogue, though the world may cast us out, we will *never* be cast out by Christ.

As we wait and hope and endure through the trials of being rejected, cast out, and hated, let us set our eyes once more on Jesus, just as the Puritans did. The tribulations may increase, and sorrows grow, but our reward in heaven is an eternal weight of glory that far outweighs all the suffering of this earth (2 Cor. 4:17).

Perhaps the best way to be prepared for whatever may come our way is to pray, with J. G. Holland, the words of this poem:

> GOD, give us men! A time like this demands
> Strong minds, great hearts, true faith and ready hands;
> Men whom the lust of office does not kill;
> Men whom the spoils of office can not buy;
> Men who possess opinions and a will;
> Men who have honor; men who will not lie;
> Men who can stand before a demagogue
> And damn his treacherous flatteries without winking!
> Tall men, sun-crowned, who live above the fog
> In public duty, and in private thinking;
> For while the rabble, with their thumb-worn creeds,
> Their large professions and their little deeds,
> Mingle in selfish strife, lo! Freedom weeps,
> Wrong rules the land and waiting Justice sleeps.[8] Amen.

---

8. Josiah Gilbert Holland, *Garnered Sheaves: The Complete Poetical Works* (New York: Scribner, Armstrong & Co., 1873), 377.

Study Questions

1. Why were the Puritans ejected from their churches on August 24, 1662, and what lesson does this teach us about following Jesus?

2. Consider the blind man of John 9. What comforting truths may we draw from his life when we're found to be living as outcasts in this world?

3. What is earthly mindedness and why is it so very dangerous for the Christian?

4. Why did the Puritans, or men like George Whitefield, keep preaching even when others hated them for it? How may this encourage us to live as Christian outcasts and pilgrims?

5. As we wait and hope as pilgrims, outcasts, and vagabonds, how do we fight the temptations to behave fearfully, insecurely, or earthly minded?

Chapter 7

Clinging to God's Promises in Sickness

I can still remember the day the message came through. I was playing with my son on the living room floor, having just finished lunch, when my phone vibrated. I pulled it out and read the dreaded words, "Your father has stage 4 lung cancer. It metastasized. They gave him weeks. We're seeking a second opinion."

"*My* dad?" I thought. "*My* dad has cancer?"

We all have different ways of responding to bad news. Sickness is no different. Whether it is about us or our loved ones, whenever a report of illness comes through, no matter the severity, we can respond either in fear or with hope. But the one thing we cannot do is ignore it.

Today many people would rather ignore sickness and death than acknowledge its existence. But we can no more successfully ignore sickness and death than a driver can ignore oncoming traffic. Sure, you may be successful at ignoring it for some time, but eventually, you're going to crash into it somewhere along the way.

This, I think, is an area where our spiritual ancestors had a leg up on us. Up until very recently, most of our ancestors confronted sickness and death daily. In some cultures, death was so familiar that when a loved one died, the body would be kept within the family's home for several days so everyone who desired to do so could come and pay their respects to the departed. Today we don't even allow families to see the coffins housing their loved ones' bodies lowered into the ground. We go to great lengths to ignore sickness and death, and yet they still come.

Of course, Christians should be some of the last people on earth trying to ignore sickness and death. The Bible speaks plainly to the reality that, because of the fall of man into sin, this world is not as it was intended to be. We understand that "the last enemy that shall be destroyed is death" (1 Cor. 15:26), but we live in the already/not yet. Christ has *already* ascended into heaven and is ruling the cosmos, awaiting the moment when all things will be made a footstool beneath His feet (Ps. 110:1; Heb. 10:13), but this has not completely happened *yet*. It most assuredly *will* happen, though. Death will be defeated. And when the trumpet sounds that Christ's triumphant victory is complete, we can rest in the sweet assurance that there will be no more pestilence, no more disease, no more sickness, no more *death*.

But until that day comes, we must be prepared to deal with sickness and illness. From common colds to sinus infections, from broken bones to cancer, from heart disease to diabetes, from heart attacks to dementia, everyone deals with sickness and disease. When this happens, we ought not to treat it as some surprising thing, nor should we be fearful of it happening or quake when it comes to pass. It is not strange or unusual, in this current order of things, for people to get sick.

Timothy was often sick, and the apostle Paul urged him to drink a little wine to help with his stomach (1 Tim. 5:23).

King Hezekiah was diagnosed with a terminal disease before God extended the length of his years (2 Kings 20:5–6).

Martin Luther was (allegedly) a worrying hypochondriac who dealt with various sicknesses on a regular basis.

Christians get sick too. There is absolutely no avoiding this. To expect otherwise is to set ourselves up for disappointment. Every one of us has had to deal with sickness and disease from birth to death.

But even sickness and disease can be endured for the glory of God. Indeed, we can wait and hope through sickness for the day when the Lord will restore our health and take away the possibility of our ever being sick again. There is a future hope of a most glorious physical resurrection on a newly remade earth, which all Christians must embrace.

The question is, How do we wait and hope even in sickness?

A Holy Example

We have already seen how the Puritans were no strangers to sickness. Cotton Mather lost *twelve* of his children and *two* of his wives to sickness, yet he set his hope firmly on the Lord. We have also seen how Jonathan Edwards, infected with smallpox, met death with both hope in Christ and peace in the assurance of salvation so that his attending physician could not help but comment that he had never before witnessed a man die with such peace. Both men are wonderful examples.

Many other Puritan are examples of courage, hope, and joy amid sickness. We will turn to some of their writings in a moment. However, before we do, one of my own heroes of the faith—Robert Murray M'Cheyne—exemplified the Puritan spirit of hope in the midst of sickness during the 1800s, and we would do well to learn from him.

Though technically not a Puritan, one would be hard-pressed to call him anything else when reading his writings. He was a young man anointed by the Holy Spirit of God and radiating His power in joy and fervency through his preaching and pastoral ministry.

M'Cheyne was born in Edinburgh, Scotland, on May 21, 1813. The son of Adam and Lockhart, his family was better off than many others, for his father not only was a lawyer but also served and brought civil cases before the Court of Session—the supreme court of Scotland. But those family riches were incomparable to the riches that became Robert's when he came to saving faith in Christ.

The catalyst for M'Cheyne's salvation was the departure of his brother William to serve as a physician with the Bengal Medical Service in India in April 1831. A few months later, his oldest brother, David, died on July 8, 1831.

Though William's journey overseas was difficult for Robert, even more heartbreaking was his brother David's departure from this world. But through death and loss came life and gain. God was pleased to use these most devastating circumstances to draw Robert Murray M'Cheyne to salvation. After his brother's passing, Robert read David Dickson and James Durham's *The Sum of Saving*

Knowledge, which seems to have been the gospel tool the Lord used to draw M'Cheyne to Christ.

For the next several years, the Lord would prepare M'Cheyne for gospel ministry. He was a well-loved and well-respected minister of the gospel who experienced wonderful revival. In fact, it was precisely because of this inner revival, and a desire to become a carrier of the gospel to foreign nations, that led him to pursue his next step of becoming a missionary.

Sickness, however, became a staple of M'Cheyne's life, which he welcomed as the reproving, sharpening, and shaping tools of the Lord. In fact, Jordan Stone wrote that "sickness, a constant companion through Robert's life, disrupted his ministry in December of 1835, just weeks after he began his parish work."[1] The doctor diagnosed him with the early stages of tuberculosis, claiming, at the same time, that his right lung was barely working.[2]

How did M'Cheyne react? Stone continues, "He always sought to discover God's providence amidst the affliction; he believed his continued struggle with illness was his Father's discipline, and this occasion was God's chastisement for being 'too anxious to do great things.'"[3] He saw a temptation toward pride within himself, and sickness both humbled him and caused him to rely on Christ. In turn, this would cause him to make much of Christ. He concluded, "*I see a man cannot be a faithful minister, until he preaches Christ for Christ's sake*—until he gives up striving to attract people to himself, and seeks only to attract them to Christ. Lord, give me this!"[4]

The Lord would answer that plea. After M'Cheyne eventually settled in as the pastor of St. Peter's in Dundee, he felt a call to reach the Jews. Traveling to Palestine, he entrusted the pulpit of St. Peter's to the young William Chalmers Burns.

---

1. Jordan Stone, *A Holy Minister: The Life and Spiritual Legacy of Robert Murray M'Cheyne* (Fearn, Scotland: Mentor, 2021), 33.

2. Stone, *Holy Minister*.

3. Stone, *Holy Minister*. See also Andrew Bonar, *Memoir and Remains of the Rev. Robert Murray M'Cheyne* (1844; repr., Edinburgh: Banner of Truth, 2012), 36.

4. Stone, *Holy Minister*. See also Bonar, *Memoir and Remains*, 43. The emphasis is in both Stone's work and Bonar's.

God did wonderful things while M'Cheyne was away. First, Burns actually experienced an incredible awakening and revival in Kilsyth in July 1839. Then, traveling back to Dundee in August, revival broke out there as well. Interestingly, Stone records that "Burns returned to Dundee on Thursday, 8 August. M'Cheyne lay flat on his bed that very day, suffering from sickness. The Spirit moved him to intercede for his flock at St. Peter's."[5] God faithfully answered M'Cheyne's prayer as he lay in his bed. Hundreds were moved to tears under Burns's preaching that same day. When M'Cheyne returned in November, he was met with a church full of souls hungry for the Word of God, Christ, and the life of God in the soul of man. This revival would then continue for the better part of the year.

Stone writes about another occasion, when, "during one prolonged period of illness, he told his sister Eliza that God had sent the disease 'to teach me that He can save and feed the people without any help of mine.'"[6] The young minister was right. God may use sickness in our lives to teach us many lessons. Sometimes, the Lord will use sickness simply to reorient our desires. It is not ambition itself that is bad but rather ambition for vain glory and self-promotion. For M'Cheyne, sickness was an opportunity to redirect and reorient his desires toward God so that his ambitions would be for His glory and His kingdom rather than the promotion of self and the applause of men.

In fact, God continually taught M'Cheyne through his seemingly constant illnesses to be a humble man of prayer who both depended on God and recognized he offered nothing to the Lord that the Lord could not supply Himself. This turned M'Cheyne into a true lover of God, who recognized the Lord's sovereignty in all things.

Eventually, M'Cheyne fell ill for the final time, as we all one day will. It was March of 1843, and he was diagnosed with typhus fever. His final sermon was preached on Sunday, March 12. Thirteen days

---

5. Stone, *Holy Minister*, 41.
6. Stone, *Holy Minister*, 69. See also Robert Murray M'Cheyne, *Familiar Letters of the Rev. Robert Murray M'Cheyne: Containing an Account of His Travels as One of the Deputation Sent Out by the Church of Scotland on a Mission of Inquiry to the Jews in 1839*, ed. Adam M'Cheyne (Robert Carter, 1849), 134–45.

later, after being bedridden, he passed away into glory on March 25, 1843, not yet having celebrated his thirtieth birthday.

Less than thirty years is what the Lord had allotted to M'Cheyne. Of those years, many of his days and hours were filled with sickness and illness. Were these punishments? M'Cheyne didn't think so. The young man once wrote, "It has always been my aim, and it is my prayer, to have *no plans* with regard to myself, well assured as I am, that the place where the Saviour sees meet to place me must ever be the best place for me."[7] He trusted in God and saw sickness as just another aspect of the sovereignty of God. If the Lord's good and gracious plans called for M'Cheyne to fall ill, then what of it? He would willingly accept it as just that: part of God's good and gracious plans.

Many may feel compelled to look at M'Cheyne's life as tragic, but that would miss the point entirely. His life was not tragic; it was filled with the grace of God. How could a man, less than thirty years of age and almost always sick, have accomplished so much for the kingdom of God? Simply by the grace of God. As Stone wrote, "'His precious life was short,' one column recalled, 'but he was an aged saint in Christian experience…into those few years there was compressed a life-time of ministerial usefulness.'"[8] Let it be said of us, no matter our age, that we are saints in Christian experience. Let it be said of us that in us lies an entire lifetime of Christian usefulness.

When sickness comes, let us follow the example of M'Cheyne and seize it as an opportunity to prayerfully trust in God and humbly depend on Him.

Responding to Sickness with the Puritans

I pray the above account of M'Cheyne's life will help us to see both that Christians *do* get sick and that God has providential purposes behind our sicknesses that we may not see ourselves. For example, could M'Cheyne have possibly known at the time that as he lay sick on his bed on August 8, 1839, praying for the congregation of St. Peter's, that the Lord was preparing the people for a great work of spiritual

---

7. Marcus Loane, *They Were Pilgrims* (Edinburgh: Banner of Truth, 2006), 147.
8. Stone, *Holy Minister*, 44.

awakening and revival? God always orchestrates the events of our lives in such a way that we end up in the exact spot He has ordained for us to be, doing the exact thing He has ordained for us to do.

Yes, God used sickness in M'Cheyne's life to bring about His mighty purposes. So it is with us. We can endure even sickness with hope because we know that God truly does work all things for our good and His glory (Rom. 8:28). We must not make the foolish error that so many others do, believing that Christians cannot get sick. Neither must we accept the lie that sickness is some strange occurrence for the Christian, for as long as we live in these mortal bodies of flesh, until the dawn of the new creation when Christ returns in triumphant glory, sickness will be a part of our existence.

The Bible is replete with both promises and commandments for the sick because it presupposes that the saints will, on occasion, fall ill. Thomas Manton, in an exposition of James 5:16 ("Confess your faults one to another, and pray one for another, that ye may be healed. The effectual fervent prayer of a righteous man availeth much."), wrote, "Christ's worshipers are not exempted from sickness, no more than any other affliction. God may chasten those whom he loveth. It is said, John xi. 3, 'Behold he whom thou lovest is sick.' Those that are dear to God have their share of miseries…it is usual in providence that they who have God's heart should feel God's hand most heavy."[9]

None are exempted from sickness. On occasion, God will even use sickness as a chastening rod on us. But ultimately, sickness should not cause us to doubt the love of God for us, though it very often does. Manton observed that "God's children never question his love so much as in sickness; our thoughts return upon us in such retirement, and the weakness of the body discomposeth the mind, and depriveth us of the free exercise of spiritual reason; to sense and feeling all is sharp. Besides, in sickness we have not that express comfort from Christ's sufferings which we have in other troubles."[10]

---

9. Thomas Manton, *An Exposition, with Notes, upon the Epistle of James*, in *The Complete Works of Thomas Manton* (1872; repr., Edinburgh: Banner of Truth, 2020), 4:450.

10. Manton, *Epistle of James*.

The key for saints, when going through a trial of affliction, is to remember that God's hands are forever enwrapped around them (John 10:28–30). They cannot be taken from His hands. They cannot be plucked away. They may look to Jesus as an ever-faithful example, "For we have not an high priest which cannot be touched with the feeling of our infirmities; but was in all points tempted like as we are, yet without sin" (Heb. 4:15). Jesus truly did suffer from sickness, and His suffering at Calvary is the proof that He endured long and hard physical afflictions on our behalf. Despite our worries and doubts, Christ *knows* what we suffer. As Manton explained,

> It is a sweet help to the thoughts when we can see that Christ went through every miserable condition to which we are exposed. Now, Christ endured want, nakedness, trouble, reproach, injustice, &c., and not sickness. Ay! But he had passions like sickness, hunger, thirst, and weariness, wherewith his body was afflicted. Christ, by experience, knoweth what it is to be under the pains and inconveniences of the Body. But if you have not the example of Christ, you have the example of all the saints.[11]

Do not let your thoughts or feelings deceive you. Christ *knows* what it is to battle through sickness. He is your example. He is your intercessor. You must, with hope, look to Him.

Even if sickness *is* a sign of God's chastisement and discipline on us, we don't stop looking to Jesus. Though Jesus was never chastised (He was, after all, sinless), He is still our example in such afflictions, for He reveals the way we can suffer afflictions with hope.

Yes, sometimes, sickness is an affliction sent on us because of sin. God lifts the chastising rod of affliction against us to draw us to repentance. If this be the case for your physical ailments, then rejoice! Your heavenly Father loves you yet and will not permit you to continue in your dreadful sins.

Sometimes, though, sickness is permitted and sent for numerous other reasons not directly related to any particular sins we have committed. Sometimes God has secret providential purposes behind our

---

11. Manton, *Epistle of James*.

physical afflictions. Think of it this way: M'Cheyne was afflicted with sickness but remained a powerful vessel in the hands of God. So too were men like Charles Spurgeon (who struggled with depression), Martin Luther, and even John Calvin.

Speaking of Calvin, Manton noted that "he was indeed a man of an indefatigable industry, but of a sickly weak body; and the same hath befallen many of the precious servants of the Lord."[12] Is it not often the case that God does the most extraordinary things through the weakest vessels? Be of good cheer, afflicted saint! The Potter may still make great use of you yet, far beyond your measure or worth!

Now we know that waiting with hope on God amid sickness and disease is an exercise in patience. Nonetheless, it can be done. Lewis Bayly's *The Practice of Piety* is extremely helpful on this account, for it includes a lengthy section titled "Meditations for the Sick." Within it he lists ten reasons why God may permit sickness within our lives, and it is vital that we recognize and remember these truths in our own lives:

> 1. That by afflictions God may not only correct our sins past, but also work in us a deeper loathing of our natural corruptions, and so prevent us from falling into many other sins, which otherwise we would commit.... With one cross God makes two cures—the chastisement of sins past, and the prevention of sin to come. For though the eternal punishment of sin, as it proceeds from justice, is fully pardoned in the sacrifice of Christ, yet we are not, without serious judging ourselves, exempted from the temporal chastisement of sin; for this proceeds only from the love of God, for our good.
>
> 2. God sends affliction to seal unto us our adoption, for "the Lord disciplines those he loves, and he punishes everyone he accepts as a son...."
>
> 3. God sends affliction to wean our hearts from too much loving this world and worldly vanities; and to cause us the more earnestly to desire and long for eternal life.

---

12. Manton, *Epistle of James*, 451.

4. By affliction and sickness God exercises his children, and the graces which he bestows upon them. He refines and tries their faith, as the goldsmith does his gold in the furnace—to make it shine more glistening and brightly (1 Pet 1:7).

5. God sends afflictions, to demonstrate to the world the trueness of his children's love and service.

6. Sanctified affliction is a singular help to further our true conversion, and to drive us home by repentance to our heavenly Father.

7. Affliction works in us pity and compassion toward our fellow-brethren that are in distress and misery.

8. God uses our sicknesses and afflictions as means and examples both to manifest to others the faith and virtues which he has bestowed upon us, as also to strengthen those who have not received so great a measure of faith as we; for there can be no greater encouragement to a weak Christian, than to behold a true Christian in the extreme sickness of his body, supported with greater patience and consolation in his soul.

9. By afflictions God makes us conformable to the image of Christ his Son (Rom 8:18; 1 Pet 4:14), who being the captain of our salvation, was made perfect through sufferings (Heb 2:10).

10. Lastly, that the godly may be humbled in respect of their own state and misery; and God glorified by delivering them out of their troubles and afflictions, when they call upon him for his help and support.[13]

Let it be a mark of great hope and encouragement that, though Bayly listed ten reason for why God may permit sickness, we could list dozens more. The truth is that we don't always know what God is doing, for we do not know His secret providences. As Deuteronomy

---

13. Lewis Bayly, *The Practice of Piety: Directing a Christian How to Walk, That He May Please God* (Morgan, Pa.: Soli Deo Gloria, 1902), 273–78.

29:29 succinctly put it, "The secret things belong unto the LORD our God: but those things which are revealed belong unto us and to our children for ever, that we may do all the words of this law." Nonetheless, we can look to the reasons that Bayly lists, or some of the examples we have seen throughout this chapter, and endure afflictions with hope.

Like the apostle Paul, it is my prayer for the one reading this that "the God of hope [will] fill you with all joy and peace in believing, that ye may abound in hope, through the power of the Holy Ghost" (Rom. 15:13).

Waiting and Hoping in Sickness

What conclusion may we draw from all we have seen? Simply this: we must look to Christ.

This may seem to be a point often repeated in this book, yet it is so incredibly vital that it may as well be printed on every page. Christ alone is your hope, your assurance, your example, your intercessor, your confidence, and your rest. If you have Christ, then you have everything you need.

When you are sick, look to Christ! He is your Great Physician. When your loved one is sick, look to Christ! He has balm for both you in your worry and the afflicted in their sickness alike. Jeremiah Burroughs wrote, "Ordinarily when we are burdened with outward afflictions, we only think of natural helps and comforts. Whereas the way for us to sanctify God's name, to do what is acceptable to God when any outward affliction comes, is to exercise our faith in the great promise of God in Jesus Christ, upon the great Covenant of Grace that God has made with us in him."[14]

Yes, let us look to Jesus even amid sickness and be comforted in the knowledge of the covenant of grace He has made with us through His blood:

---

14. Jeremiah Burroughs, *The Wonders of Jesus* (Crossville, Tenn.: Puritan Publications, 2022), 21.

Eternal and merciful God and Father, the eternal salvation of the living and the eternal life of the dying, You alone have life and death in Your hands. You continually care for us in such a way that neither health nor sickness, neither good nor evil, can befall us—indeed, not even a hair can fall from our heads—without Your will. You order all things for the good of believers.

We ask that You will grant us the grace of the Holy Spirit, that He may teach us to know truly our miseries, and to bear patiently Your chastisements, which, as far as our merits are concerned, might have been ten thousand times more severe. We know that they are not tokens of Your wrath, but of Your fatherly love for us, that we might not be condemned with the world.

Increase our faith by Your Holy Spirit, that we may become more and more united with Christ, to whom You desire to conform us, both in suffering and in glory. Lighten our cross, so that we in our weakness may be able to bear it. We submit ourselves without reserve to Your holy will, whether You leave our souls here in these earthly tents or take them home to Yourself. We have no fear, because we belong to Christ and therefore shall not perish. We even desire to depart from this weak body in the hope of a blessed resurrection, knowing that then it will be restored to us in a much more glorious form.[15] Amen.

---

15. "Prayer for the Sick and Spiritually Distressed—2," in *Liturgical Forms and Prayers of the United Reformed Churches in North America together with the Doctrinal Standards of URCNA* (Wellandport, Ontario: United Reformed Church in North America, 2018), 119–20.

Study Questions

1. What is your natural inclination when it comes to responding to bad news?

2. How did God use M'Cheyne's sickness for his good and God's glory?

3. What is the cause of sickness and how should we (biblically) respond to it?

4. In what ways may God use affliction in our lives as Christians?

5. Lewis Bayly offers numerous reasons for why God may permit sickness in the lives of Christians. With these in mind, how may we patiently wait on the Lord and hope in His promises when we are battling affliction (whether physically, mentally, or spiritually)?

Chapter 8

When Death Calls Us Home

It has been said that the great equalizer is death. All men, whether rich or poor, powerful or powerless, will die.

Though many today would accuse Christians of having a weak view of death, Scripture speaks both often and brazenly about the death of the Christian. And, perhaps unsurprisingly, it does so in joyous terms. For the Christian, death is not a moment to fear, but to look forward to; not a moment to avoid, but to embrace when it comes. For, when the Christian dies, he is closer to the Lord than ever before. In that sweet moment of death, Christians are transported from this old world of sin and darkness and into Christ's eternal kingdom and presence. What was begun at the moment of salvation will be completed when the departed saints, who abide now with Christ to await their future resurrection, are gloriously resurrected when Christ returns to the earth in glory to consummate His kingdom on the new heaven and new earth. There is nothing greater than this.

Puritan Examples of Hope Even in Death
All who have come before us have died. All who live alongside us now will die. This is inescapable. As the writer of Ecclesiastes put it, both the righteous and the wicked will face death one day:

> For all this I considered in my heart even to declare all this, that the righteous, and the wise, and their works, are in the hand of God: no man knoweth either love or hatred by all that is before them. All things come alike to all: there is one event to the

righteous, and to the wicked; to the good and to the clean, and to the unclean; to him that sacrificeth, and to him that sacrificeth not: as is the good, so is the sinner; and he that sweareth, as he that feareth an oath. This is an evil among all things that are done under the sun, that there is one event unto all: yea, also the heart of the sons of men is full of evil, and madness is in their heart while they live, and after that they go to the dead. (Eccl. 9:1–3)

The Puritans were themselves no strangers to death and wrote about it often. They knew the truth that not all sickness will lead to death, but some sickness will. Not every danger will cause us to perish, but some danger may. This may be the day we draw our final breath and die, or it may not be. Ultimately, we must trust God and not worry about what the future holds. If we are truly held in the hands of a sovereign God, then we need not fret nor fear the future. Even death itself may be met with joy, laughter, and mirth.

We must not fret ourselves with worry over death; instead, we must trust the good purposes of our God. Consider the words of John Owen, who said, "The eternal love of God towards his elect is nothing but his purpose, good pleasure, a pure act of his will, whereby he determines to do such and such things for them in his own time and way."[1] God has good purposes behind all that happens within our lives. Even death has a place in God's grand design for us, though death will not always have a place in eternity. Nonetheless, we can trust God's purposes, just like Owen and the other Puritans.

This is why it is so important we grasp what Jesus said in Luke 12:22–32:

> Therefore I say unto you, Take no thought for your life, what ye shall eat; neither for the body, what ye shall put on. The life is more than meat, and the body is more than raiment.
> Consider the ravens: for they neither sow nor reap; which neither have storehouse nor barn; and God feedeth them: how much more are ye better than the fowls? And which of you with

---

1. John Owen, *The Death of Death in the Death of Christ* (repr., Edinburgh: Banner of Truth, 1959), 164.

taking thought can add to his stature one cubit? If ye then be not able to do that thing which is least, why take ye thought for the rest? Consider the lilies how they grow: they toil not, they spin not; and yet I say unto you, that Solomon in all his glory was not arrayed like one of these. If then God so clothe the grass, which is to day in the field, and to morrow is cast into the oven; how much more will he clothe you, O ye of little faith? And seek not ye what ye shall eat, or what ye shall drink, neither be ye of doubtful mind. For all these things do the nations of the world seek after: and your Father knoweth that ye have need of these things. But rather seek ye the kingdom of God; and all these things shall be added unto you. Fear not, little flock; for it is your Father's good pleasure to give you the kingdom.

We see God's "good pleasure to give [us] the kingdom" within this text, and so we know that His purposes for us are good. If we die, we will have great gain as we step foot into heavenly glory to be with the Lord forever, and if we live, we have a chance to live as ambassadors for Christ and His kingdom on this earth. In each instance, we can serve and glorify God. Death must not be seen as an end of our service to Christ or the close of our life's book. Rather, death simply marks the end of our story's prologue. The rest is yet to come in eternity, written in a book that has *no* end.

For those of us who are suffering because of a loved one's impending death, or who are facing death themselves, or who have lost loved ones already, there are a few things that must be done if we desire to wait on God for the day of future resurrection with hope. Namely, we must learn how *not* to be anxious over death. We must learn not to fear it. We must learn, as the Puritans did, to approach death with an inexhaustible hope.

We Must Not Fear Death
Many fear death, but it is not fitting for a Christian to do so. We ought instead to have confidence in the triumphant victory of Christ over death. Athanasius, the early church father, taught brilliantly on the death of death in Christ in *On the Incarnation,* wherein he declared,

If, then, it is by the sign of the cross and by faith in Christ that death is trampled underfoot, it is clear that it is Christ Himself and none other Who is the Archvictor over death and has robbed it of its power. Death used to be strong and terrible, but now, since the sojourn of the Saviour and the death and resurrection of His body, it is despised; and obviously it is by the very Christ Who mounted on the cross that it has been destroyed and vanquished finally. When the sun rises after the night and the whole world is lit up by it, nobody doubts that it is the sun which has thus shed its light everywhere and driven away the dark. Equally clear is it, since this utter scorning and trampling down of death has ensued upon the Saviour's manifestation in the body and His death on the cross, that it is He Himself Who brought death to nought and daily raises monuments to His victory in His own disciples.[2]

We must know that Christ is victorious over death and so approach death with hope. Jesus has removed death's sting, as the venom is removed from a snake. It may bite, but it will not permanently disable the saint. Because of Adam and Eve's transgression, we will die, but death cannot hold us in the grave. Rather, we immediately go into the presence of our Lord with the promise that, one day, our bodies will be resurrected and glorified on a new earth. No matter how much time passes, no matter the state of our bodies at that point, the Lord will resurrect us. Death will not have the final say.

This is the way Thomas Shepard approached death. One of the foremost Puritans to come to the New England colonies, he had been a source of tension within the Church of England when he angered Archbishop William Laud with his preaching. Coming to New England then in 1635, he spent some years as a missionary to the Native Americans. In Cambridge, Massachusetts, he would both pastor and serve at the newly founded Harvard University, then designed to train up Puritan ministers.

---

2. Athanasius, *On the Incarnation*, trans. a religious of C.S.M.V. S.Th. (Louisville, Ky.: GLH Publishing, 2018), 22. Kindle Edition.

Then, suddenly, he was dying. He was on his deathbed at only forty-four years old. What began as a sore throat proved fatal when, on August 25, 1649, he entered glory. How would Shepard meet death? What would he say? What would he do?

It was in the final days of his life that he penned these beautiful words:

> O my sinful heart! O my often-crucified but never wholly mortified sinfulness! O my life-long damage and my daily shame! O my indwelling and so besetting sins, your evil dominions is over now! It is now within an hour or two of my final and everlasting release! For I am authoritatively assured that by to-morrow morning I shall have entered into my eternal rest! And then, I my ransomed soul, one hour in heaven will make me forget all my hell upon earth![3]

How did Shepard die? With hope! He knew that one moment with Jesus in glory would wash away all the trials of this life, and he gladly embraced death as the gateway to paradise.

We Must Trust That God Has Appointed the Hour of Our Death

Many live their days in a constant fear of death. Some are so frightened and afraid of dying, they go to extreme measures and take incredible precautions to try and stall death for just a little while longer. We are often tempted to pray for health and well-being for ourselves and our families—which is a perfectly fine prayer to pray, except when we make the luxuries of health and well-being idols in our lives. We must remember that suffering produces godly growth in our lives. Even death produces godliness, for as a seed must die in the ground before sprouting forth in new life, so the saint must lay their sin-corrupted and mortal body in the ground before experiencing the fullness of everlasting life. As Jesus said,

> Verily, verily, I say unto you, Except a corn of wheat fall into the ground and die, it abideth alone: but if it die, it bringeth forth much fruit. He that loveth his life shall lose it; and he that hateth

---

3. Benge and Pickowicz, *American Puritans*, 112.

his life in this world shall keep it unto life eternal. If any man serve me, let him follow me; and where I am, there shall also my servant be: if any man serve me, him will my Father honour. (John 12:24–26)

The temptation to put health and well-being on a pedestal is a real one, but it's a trap we must not fall for. The tendency to worry and fret and try our best to extend our lives is common to human experience, but such worry is sinful. This is, in a sense, exactly what Jesus was saying not to do. If God clothes the lily of the field, feeds the raven of the air, and cares for things that are seemingly small and tiny, won't He most assuredly care for us?

Jesus told us that the Father's care for us is certain; in fact, the Father has promised us a place in His kingdom! We need not fear or worry about death. Rather, we can trust that whatever God ordains is right. After all, Jesus has promised our every need will be supplied. If the need is for us to keep living, then God will supply everything needed for that to happen. If the need is that we die, then God will supply everything necessary to make that happen.

To approach death with trust in God means that Paul's words in Acts 20:24 ought to ring true for us all: "None of these things move me, neither count I my life dear unto myself, so that I might finish my course with joy, and the ministry, which I have received of the Lord Jesus, to testify the gospel of the grace of God." To trust God in death means we ought to remember that "to live is Christ, and to die is gain" (Phil. 1:21), and so, "whether we live, we live unto the Lord; and whether we die, we die unto the Lord: whether we live therefore, or die, we are the Lord's" (Rom. 14:8).

Men like Martin Luther and John Bunyan bravely faced death when it came to them. In fact, both men died under similar circumstances. Both had traveled from home to go and minister to others engaged in conflict. Both became ill while trying to reconcile warring parties. And both then died from their illnesses. But, most importantly, neither man counted his life dear to himself, but trusted that God would faithfully use him as He determined. Is this not the testimony of every saint, Puritan or not, who trusts God's good purposes rather than worrying and fretting over a day and hour we have no control over?

John Paton was another man with a similarly hopeful disposition toward death. A Scottish Protestant missionary to the New Hebrides Islands in the South Pacific in the nineteenth century, he exemplified trust in God on many extraordinary occasions, like the time cannibals came to his tiny hut, demanding he turn himself over to them. But it was on another occasion, when his life was being threatened, that he came to realize how important it is to trust the sovereignty of God over our lives:

> They encircled us in a deadly ring, and one kept urging another to strike the first blow or fire the first shot. My heart rose up to the Lord Jesus; I saw Him watching all the scene. My peace came back to me like a wave from God. I realized that I was immortal till my Master's work with me was done. The assurance came to me, as if a voice out of Heaven had spoken, that not a musket would be fired to wound us, not a club prevail to strike us, not a spear leave the hand in which it was held vibrating to be thrown, not an arrow leave the bow, or a killing stone the fingers, without the permission of Jesus Christ, whose is all power in Heaven and on Earth. He rules all Nature, animate and inanimate, and restrains even the Savage of the South Seas. In that awful hour I saw His own words, as if carved in letters of fire upon the clouds of Heaven: "Seek, and ye shall find. Whatsoever ye shall ask in My Name, that will I do, that the Father may be glorified in the Son." I could understand how Stephen and John saw the glorified Savior as they gazed up through suffering and persecution to the Heavenly Throne![4]

Immortal until God's work is done, indeed. The Lord has numbered our days, and we will not shorten them by a single second less or lengthen them by a single moment more. Has worrying ever added a second to anyone's life? We must simply trust that God, in His good providence, will call us to Himself at the appointed time. When we

---

4. John G. Paton, *Missionary to the New Hebrides: An Autobiography* (Edinburgh: Banner of Truth; 1994), 207.

close our eyes for the final time here, we will immediately open them in the presence of our Savior. This is the earnest hope and expectation of all who call Christ their Savior and Lord.

Poetic Reminders of the Puritan Hope Even in Death

While the writings of the Puritans are replete with words of encouragement for the one facing death or grieving a loved one, perhaps no pen speaks more poetically and soul-stirringly of death than that of John Donne. He was born into a recusant family in London in 1572; his Roman Catholic family members refused to attend worship services held by the Church of England—that is, until 1610 when he began to publish anti-Catholic pamphlets. Since he would then join and remain a part of the Church of England, the technical label of Puritan may not apply to him as it would many of the saints we've examined thus far. However, he did possess that indomitable Puritan spirit that was peculiar to the age, permitting him to rebel against spiritual wickedness with the wit, wisdom, and fervor of genuine Christian holiness.

Eventually, Donne became a cleric within the Church of England, being ordained as a deacon in 1615 and later as a priest. Though it has been said that preaching took a deathly physical toll on Donne, with every preached sermon more difficult than the last, he preached a number of sermons that have survived, including his famous "Death's Duel," delivered February 25, 1631, before King Charles I at the Palace of Whitehall. In it, he considers how all men will die; how all men must die. With vivid language, he considers death and the grave with vivid clarity. But he concludes with hope: "There we leave you in that blessed dependency, to hang upon him that hangs upon the cross, there bathe in his tears, there suck at his wounds, and lie down in peace in his grave, till he vouchsafe you a resurrection, and an ascension into that kingdom which He hath prepared for you with the inestimable price of his incorruptible blood. Amen."[5]

---

5. John Donne, "Death's Duel," Christian Classics Ethereal Library, accessed December 2, 2023, https://www.ccel.org/ccel/donne/deaths_duel.html.

As fine a preacher as he seems to have been, it's his poems for which he is most remembered today. One, "Death Be Not Proud," contains some of the most theologically rich language any Christian has penned about death:

> Death, be not proud, though some have called thee
> Mighty and dreadful, for thou art not so;
> For those whom thou think'st thou dost overthrow
> Die not, poor Death, nor yet canst thou kill me.
> From rest and sleep, which but thy pictures be,
> Much pleasure; then from thee much more must flow,
> And soonest our best men with thee do go,
> Rest of their bones, and soul's delivery.
> Thou art slave to fate, chance, kings, and desperate men,
> And dost with poison, war, and sickness dwell,
> And poppy or charms can make us sleep as well
> And better than thy stroke; why swell'st thou then?
> One short sleep past, we wake eternally
> And death shall be no more; Death, thou shalt die.[6]

Yes, truly, death shall die. It remains the final enemy, but it shall most certainly die because Jesus is "the resurrection, and the life" and has promised that "he that believeth in me, though he were dead, yet shall he live" (John 11:25).

Waiting with Hope in Death
J. R. R. Tolkien's *The Lord of the Rings* is a work that needs no introduction. Less than a century after its publication, it is already considered a modern literary classic, and for good reason. It's extremely well written, with memorable characters and some of the most beautiful scenes and prose ever put to paper. It also handles death in a fascinating way.

Unsurprisingly, Tolkien's characters grapple with tribulation, trial, suffering, and death in their adventure to destroy the Ring of

---

6. John Donne, "Holy Sonnets: Death, Be Not Proud," Poetry Foundation, accessed December 2, 2023, https://www.poetryfoundation.org/poems/44107/holy-sonnets-death-be-not-proud.

Power and defeat the dark lord Sauron. One line has always stood out to me in this regard: "Faithless is he that says farewell when the road darkens."[7]

The dwarf Gimli is speaking with the half-elf, Elrond. In retrospect, perhaps it is true that the line is spoken hastily by a rash character. However, the sentence does get at the heart of the matter for the Christian: when the path is blanketed by shadows, uncertainties plague the future, and it seems all but certain that the road has ended, the Christian must look up—not to the hills, for our hope does not come from there, but to heaven, where sits the Lord enthroned, who made heaven and earth.

We must not be so faithless as to believe that death is the end. For those who are in Christ, death is merely a temporary parting. We know that, in the eternity to come, we will forever be united with both the Lord and His people.

Keith and Kristyn Getty, along with Matt Papa, affirm this truth in their song "Christ Our Hope in Life and Death." Effectively, they put the first question and answer from the Heidelberg Catechism to song. In the second verse, they sing these words:

> What truth can calm the troubled soul?
> God is good, God is good.
> Where is his grace and goodness known?
> In our great Redeemer's blood.
>
> Who holds our faith when fears arise?
> Who stands above the stormy trial?
> Who sends the waves that bring us nigh
> Unto the shore, the rock of Christ?

Though the final question of that verse is not directly answered in the song, the chorus points us once more to the Father and the Son:

---

7. J. R. R. Tolkien, *The Fellowship of the Ring* (New York: Houghton Mifflin, 1993), 274.

O sing hallelujah!
Our hope springs eternal;
O sing hallelujah!
Now and ever we confess
Christ our hope in life and death.[8]

The song itself, of course, is based on the Heidelberg Catechism, that great Reformed catechism of the seventeenth century. In 1680, the English Baptist Hercules Collins took the Heidelberg Catechism and, with some small editing, updated and transformed it into the Orthodox Catechism for Particular Baptist churches. The first two questions provide a wonderful comfort to those saints facing trials in this life or facing that trial which meets us all at the end of life:

Question 1: What is thy only comfort in life and death?

Answer: That both in soul and body, whether I live or die, I am not mine own, but belong wholly unto my most faithful Lord and Saviour Jesus Christ: who by his most precious blood fully satisfying for my sins, hath delivered me from all the power of the devil, and so preserveth me, that without the will of my heavenly Father not so much as a hair may fall from my head; yea all things must serve for my safety: wherefore by his Spirit also he assureth me of everlasting life, and maketh me ready and prepared, that henceforth I may live to him.

Question 2: How many things are necessary for thee to know, that thou enjoying this comfort mayst live and die happily?

Answer: Three. The first, what is the greatness of my sin and misery. The second, how I am delivered from all sin and misery. The third, what thanks I owe unto God for this delivery.[9]

Do you know the greatness of your sin and misery apart from Christ?

---

8. "Christ Our Hope in Life and Death," Getty Music, accessed December 2, 2023, https://www.gettymusic.com/christ-our-hope.

9. Hercules Collins, *An Orthodox Catechism* (Glasgow, Scotland: Parresia, 2021), 9–11.

Do you know the greatness of your delivery from sin and misery in Christ?

Do you know to give God thanks for your deliverance in Christ?

Then, dearly beloved, be of good cheer! Not even death itself can pluck you away from Christ. He is your comfort while you live, and He will still be your comfort when you die.

This is where our theology becomes truly practical—where the rubber hits the road, as they say. Ours is a faith that requires both contemplation (theology) and action (the practical working out of theological implications and doctrines).

Theological tenets and doctrines, as gleaned from Scripture, are the tires of life. But tires are meant to touch the road. They have a very practical purpose. And so the way a Christian grapples with death is a prime example of how the rubber must meet the road eventually. A study of Scripture that does not prepare one to both live and die well for Christ is terribly impractical. Impractical theology is simply not Christian. By its very nature, Christian theology must always be practical.

Martin Bucer reflected on this and wrote, "True theology is not theoretical, but practical. The end of it is living, that is to live a Godly life."[10] We can add to this statement that true theology's end is also dying a godly death.

William Perkins, in similar fashion, famously said, "The body of Scripture is a doctrine sufficient to live well. It comprehends many holy sciences, where one is principal; others are handmaids or retainers. The principal science is theology. Theology is the science of living blessedly forever. Blessed life arises from the knowledge of God."[11]

The world uses its secular means of science to put off, stall, and thwart death. But we, as Christians, have the overarching science of theology in Scripture. It teaches us not only how to live blessedly but die blessedly.

---

10. Quoted in Brian Lugioyo, *Martin Bucer's Doctrine of Justification: Reformation Theology and Early Irenicism*, Oxford Studies in Historical Theology (Oxford: Oxford University Press, 2010), 54.

11. Perkins, *Golden Chain*, 6:11.

Yes, theology must be practical. We must be able to put it to work. Sir William Francis Butler understood this concept and principle well too. A lieutenant general in the British Army, he was also a writer of biographies. Reflecting on the danger of a philosophy that was always theoretical and never practical, he warned, "The nation that will insist on drawing a broad line of demarcation between the fighting man and the thinking man is liable to find its fighting done by fools and its thinking done by cowards."[12] Butler was saying that philosophy and fighting must never be divorced from each other. Genuine philosophy should imbue fighting with meaning and purpose, and meaning and purpose should undergird philosophy. In other words, philosophy gives meaning to the fighting, and the fighting is simply the application of philosophy. If fighting is stripped of philosophy, then there is no purpose behind it. And if philosophy can't give meaning to the fighting, it too is without purpose. To mix this up is to turn everything topsy-turvy.

So it is with theology. Theology and practice must never be divorced from each other. A theology that cannot be lived and died is impractical and therefore useless. But Christians who have God's Word always have access to the most accessible and practical tenets of theology. This means that because Christ has defeated death (theology), we need not fear it (practice). Because Christ has risen, we, too, will one day rise (theology), and we can look to death as a door that opens to glory (practice).

Another way we see theology and practice intersect is in the beautiful passage of 1 Corinthians 15:51–58. In verses 51–57 we see a theology of Christ's victory over death and a promise of future resurrection:

> Behold, I shew you a mystery; we shall not all sleep, but we shall all be changed, in a moment, in the twinkling of an eye, at the last trump: for the trumpet shall sound, and the dead shall be raised incorruptible, and we shall be changed. For this

---

12. Sir William Francis Butler, *Charles George Gordon* (London: Macmillan and Co., 1901), 85.

corruptible must put on incorruption, and this mortal must put on immortality. So when this corruptible shall have put on incorruption, and this mortal shall have put on immortality, then shall be brought to pass the saying that is written, Death is swallowed up in victory. O death, where is thy sting? O grave, where is thy victory? The sting of death is sin; and the strength of sin is the law. But thanks be to God, which giveth us the victory through our Lord Jesus Christ.

Praise God! We have victory over death in Jesus. What, then, is the practicality of these doctrines? Verse 58 spells it out: "Therefore, my beloved brethren, be ye stedfast, unmoveable, always abounding in the work of the Lord, forasmuch as ye know that your labour is not in vain in the Lord." Because of our victory over death in Christ, we must be steadfast, unmovable, abounding in our work for the Lord, trusting that our work is never in vain.

Beloved, we need not fear death. It is not vain. It has a purpose that God most certainly can utilize for our good and His glory. We can wait for our day of dying with hope because of what Christ accomplished through His death, burial, and resurrection.

Anne Bradstreet is remembered today for being one of the first English Puritans to be published in the North American colonies. Her body of work contains a vast amount of wonderful poetry. One of my favorites is her "As Weary Pilgrim, Now at Rest." Below I have recorded the second half of this poem to help lead us in prayer as we praise Jesus for the victory He has brought us over death, while longing and waiting for the fullest experience of this victory in the future resurrection to come:

> A pilgrim I, on earth, perplext
>   wth sinns wth cares and sorrows vext
> By age and paines brought to decay
>   and my Clay house mouldring away
> Oh how I long to be at rest
>   and soare on high among the blest.
> This body shall in silence sleep
>   Mine eyes no more shall ever weep

No fainting fits shall me assaile
    nor grinding paines my body fraile
Wth cares and fears ne'r cumbred be
    Nor losses know, nor sorrowes see
What tho my flesh shall there consume
    it is the bed Christ did perfume
And when a few yeares shall be gone
    this mortall shall be cloth'd vpon
A Corrupt Carcasse downe it lyes
    a glorious body it shall rise
In weaknes and dishonour sowne
    in power 'tis rais'd by Christ alone
Then soule and body shall vnite
    and of their maker haue the sight
Such lasting ioyes shall there behold
    as eare ne'r heard nor tongue e'er told
Lord make me ready for that day
    then Come deare bridgrome Come away.[13] Amen.

---

13. Anne Bradstreet, "As Weary Pilgrim, Now at Rest," Poet and Poem, accessed December 2, 2023, https://poetandpoem.com/Anne-Bradstreet/As-weary-pilgrim-now-at-rest.

Study Questions

1. What do you think of when you think of death? What does the Bible point us to when it speaks of death?

2. Read Luke 12:22–32 again. How does Jesus prepare us for both life and death with this passage?

3. How should a Christian approach the death of a loved one? How about their own death?

4. Both John Donne and J. R. R. Tolkien wrote of death in helpful and encouraging ways. What truths may we draw from their writings?

5. "And as it is appointed unto men once to die, but after this the judgment" (Heb. 9:27). How do we prepare for death? (Hint: the gospel!)

Chapter 9

When Weeping Tarries for the Night

The Monday Morning Blues.

That's what I call the feeling I sometimes get on Monday mornings. The previous Lord's Day may have gone terrifically. My preaching may have been just fine, the sermon may have been received well, and we may have enjoyed our fellowship with the saints. Yet Monday morning rolls around and, suddenly, I find myself thinking about everything that went *wrong*.

It may be that those things that went wrong were relatively small and nitpicky. Maybe no one else noticed how I stumbled over pronouncing the names in the genealogy. They most certainly cannot know how I failed to preach part of my sermon. They probably have no idea that I forgot something in my public, pastoral prayer. But I know, and the feeling can be crushing.

Or it could be I shook a hundred hands of people with smiling faces, happy to worship the Lord. Then came one more hand, and it was attached to a frowning face with a list of complaints and grievances to share. And now, as I prepare to begin a new week, this will be the thought that consumes me in the morning.

These things may seem small and trivial, but they are major causes of spiritual depression. If I don't immediately nip these things in the bud through Scripture reading, prayer, and praise, then I am almost certainly done for that morning.

It doesn't even have to be a Monday. These thoughts could come on Thursday. And they may not be connected to anything at all. I may just feel gloomy. I may be down and out for no discernible purpose.

The Puritans had a name for this. They called it "the dark night of the soul." Today we usually refer to it as "spiritual depression." It's that moment when the saint of God feels disconnected from the Lord. There is no immediate joy or comfort to be had. An uneasy feeling strikes, anxieties overwhelm, and lethargy kicks in. It feels impossible to get out of bed and start the day. In the worst of cases, tears flow, but we cannot really say why.

Whether you call it the "Monday Morning Blues," the "dark night of the soul," or "spiritual depression," every one of us will encounter it at various points as we walk through this vale of tears. Of course, this is when the battle for joy is most ferocious and, if we're honest, most important. If we give even a foothold to our enemies of the world, the flesh, and the devil, it will not be long until we are wallowing in self-pity. Becoming consumed with ourselves and our failures and shortcomings, we fail to lift our eyes to Christ to see the glorious reasons for our hope and joy.

If I had to take a wild guess, I would venture to assume that every Christian who picks up this book is going to be familiar with spiritual depression as the suffering we must endure most frequently. Sure, it may be related to the other topics we have considered, such as struggling with sin or sickness, or being persecuted or rejected. It is often the case that our periods of spiritual depression are caused or—at the very least—deepened by some sudden suffering within our lives. For those with more sensitive spirits, it may take very little indeed to bring on a bout with spiritual depression, but it is truly an affliction common to us all.

Martyn Lloyd-Jones, in his work on spiritual depression, wrote, "It is interesting to notice the frequency with which this particular theme is dealt with in the Scriptures and the only conclusion to be drawn from that is that it is a very common condition."[1] Indeed, it is so very common that many of the psalms deal explicitly with the topic, as when David began Psalm 42 with these words:

---

1. Martyn Lloyd-Jones, *Spiritual Depression: Its Causes and Cure* (Grand Rapids: Eerdmans, 1965), 10.

> As the hart panteth after the water brooks, so panteth my soul after thee, O God. My soul thirsteth for God, for the living God: when shall I come and appear before God? My tears have been my meat day and night, while they continually say unto me, Where is thy God? When I remember these things, I pour out my soul in me: for I had gone with the multitude, I went with them to the house of God, with the voice of joy and praise, with a multitude that kept holyday. Why art thou cast down, O my soul? and why art thou disquieted in me? hope thou in God: for I shall yet praise him for the help of his countenance. (vv. 1–5)

There will be times when "weeping may endure for a night" (Ps. 30:5). I am sure that every saint reading this has felt in their soul what David described in Psalm 42. While we hunger and pant after God, we seem unable to find Him. His presence seems far from us. Yet, at the same time, we know that Jesus cried out those dreadful words, "My God, my God, why hast thou forsaken me?" (Matt. 27:46) so that He could promise us, "My child, my child, I will never leave nor forsake you" (see Heb. 13:5).

It is not a lack of promises on God's behalf that cause us to become downcast in spirit, but a lack of faith. Martyn Lloyd-Jones refused to mince words when he wrote, "The ultimate cause of all spiritual depression is unbelief."[2] So, the most important starting point for the one going through "the dark night of the soul" is with the simple prayer, "I believe; help my unbelief!"

A Violent Fight for Joy

Self-help books are often full of nonsense. The idea that one may "pull themselves up by their bootstraps" may sound brave and courageous, but it's effectively impossible. Just as we rely on God to live, move, and have our being (Acts 17:28), so we rely on Him to find comfort, joy, and the strength to keep pressing on.

However, we must put effort into our fight for victory over spiritual depression. This is a battle that we must fight as part of an overarching war for joy as Christians. We must fight for joy. Weeping

---

2. Lloyd-Jones, *Spiritual Depression*, 20.

may tarry for a night, but we ought not to permit it room and board. With all the violent tenacity we can muster, we must evict and force it from our very beings, lest it sit and recline by an open hearth and make itself most comfortable, believing itself to have found a home within us.

While it is true that only the Lord can ultimately bring us victory when we are under such assaults, we have work to do too. Lloyd-Jones made the reason for this battle explicit when he wrote, "A depressed Christian is a contradiction in terms, and he is a very poor recommendation for the gospel. We are living in a pragmatic age. People today are not primarily interested in Truth but they are interested in results. The one question they ask is: Does it work? They are frantically seeking and searching for something that can help them."[3]

The gospel is very much at stake here. Men must not look to us and see within our countenance a never-ending sadness coupled with anxiety and depression. This would give others the false impression that Jesus does not satisfy or make His people eternally joyful. Men must look to us and see the truth that Christ alone eternally satisfies, and He does so truly. Thus, Lloyd-Jones continued:

> Now we believe that God extends His Kingdom partly through His people, and we know that He has oftentimes done some of the most notable things in the history of the Church through the simple Christian living of some quite ordinary people. Nothing is more important, therefore, than that we should be delivered from a condition which gives other people, looking at us, the impression that to be a Christian means to be unhappy, to be sad, to be morbid, and that the Christian is one who "scorns delights and lives laborious days."[4]

We must not lie to others. If the one whom Christ sets free is truly free (John 8:36), then we must not be marked by tears. The one who is free in Christ has been given liberty and freedom from the yoke of bondage (Gal. 5:1). No longer slaves to sin, we can now do that

---

3. Lloyd-Jones, *Spiritual Depression*, 11.
4. Lloyd-Jones, *Spiritual Depression*, 11.

which eternally satisfies—namely, glorify God—because we have been given a brand-new heart with new desires and abilities. And, as the Westminster Shorter Catechism aptly puts it in Question and Answer 1, we must glorify and enjoy God forever. Far from being two separate things, these are one and the same. The more we glorify God, the more joy we will experience as we enjoy Him; and the more joy we have in enjoying Him, the more He will be glorified by us. This joy, then, brings God glory as it points men to the truth that Christ is our eternal treasure and joy.

It is this joy that we must fight for, that others also may see it and glorify our Father in heaven (Matt. 5:16). Weeping may tarry for the night, but you must not be content with permitting it to stay the next day as well. It may seem as though it would be easier to give in to despair and quit the fight, but *souls are at stake*. The gospel is at stake. It may seem easier to succumb to spiritual depression, but it is extremely costly.

When Jael was sitting in her tent, awaiting news from Israel's battle against Jabin, king of Canaan, she may have thought it far easier to simply remain put. Rather than venture outside her tent, it surely would have been more comfortable to stay within—especially when she saw the danger lurking outside—namely, Sisera, the captain of King Jabin's army, approaching.

Jael was "the wife of Heber the Kenite" (Judg. 4:17), and there was peace between Heber and Jabin. Obviously, Sisera was now seeking refuge. Again, it may have been far easier to stay within her tent, but Jael chose instead to fight:

> And Jael went out to meet Sisera, and said unto him, Turn in, my lord, turn in to me; fear not. And when he had turned in unto her into the tent, she covered him with a mantle. And he said unto her, Give me, I pray thee, a little water to drink; for I am thirsty. And she opened a bottle of milk, and gave him drink, and covered him. Again he said unto her, Stand in the door of the tent, and it shall be, when any man doth come and enquire of thee, and say, Is there any man here? that thou shalt say, No. Then Jael Heber's wife took a nail of the tent, and took

an hammer in her hand, and went softly unto him, and smote the nail into his temples, and fastened it into the ground: for he was fast asleep and weary. So he died. (Judg. 4:18–21)

Our fight against the "dark night of the soul" may look much like this. It may be bloody, violent, and furious. It may feel as though it would be far easier to stay tucked in bed, inside our homes, permitting the enemy of despair to wash over us like a flood. But, like Jael, we must be willing to raise the tent peg and drive it through its awful head.

Thankfully, the Puritans knew a thing or two about dealing with spiritual depression, and we now turn our attention to them as we draw up our own battle plans.

Mapping the Battle Plans

Carefully consider, dear Christian, that the devil comes only to steal, kill, and destroy, while Christ comes to give, rebirth, and reanimate (John 10:10). It is no mistake that many are made afraid of coming to Christ, and it is by devilish design that a watching world should see suffering Christians and find them to be worse off than they. But let no Christian reading this suffer with a frown; whether under persecution, battling sin, suffering rejection, or in sickness, we must not lose our joy in Christ. John Flavel wrote, "It is a vile and groundless slander upon religion, to say or insinuate that it deprives men of the comfort and joy of life."[5]

This means the battle is essential *and* that we must first know the tactics of our adversary, the devil. Just how, exactly, does he work to bring about the dark night of the soul? Flavel explained that, primarily, the devil tries to keep us from coming to Christ. He tries to make us believe that most awful lie that we will find no joy in turning to Jesus:

> The devil, in design to discourage us from the ways of God, puts a frightful mask upon the beautiful face of religion, pretending there is no pleasure of joy to be expected therein; but this is abundantly confuted and refelled in the text, "I will come in to

---

5. John Flavel, *England's Duty*, in *The Works of John Flavel* (repr., Edinburgh: Banner of Truth, 2021), 4:226.

him and sup with him." Solomon tells us, Eccl. x. 19, "A feast is made for laughter." I am sure that soul that sits with Christ at such a feast as has been described above, has the best reason of any man in the world to be merry.[6]

Let's be clear, then: Christians have abundantly more reason to laugh and be joyful because we have union with Christ, and Christ has promised to feast with us. Indeed, we must feast with Christ, which is accomplished through the simple methods of prayer and study of Scripture! We certainly ought not to neglect assembling with the saints either (Heb. 10:25).

For those united to Christ, a profound joy is accentuated when we gather with other saints to lift our voices in praise. Do not permit spiritual depression to keep you from that which you need the most; you need Christ, and you need His people. Don't let the devil fool you into believing that you're better off alone.

If you're reading this but you are *not* saved, then you must quickly repent of your sins and come to Christ, who will embrace you warmly in His arms, for there is far greater joy to be found in Him than anything in this world. Flavel continued, "No man can be owner of any true comfort till he be in Christ. Comfort and refreshment, in the natural order follow faith; it is the vainest imagination in the world to expect solid, spiritual comfort before union with Christ; you may as well expect an harvest before a seed-time."[7]

If, on the other hand, you *are* saved, then read these words from Flavel carefully: "Whatever the after-sufferings of Christians may be, the worst is past when they are once in Christ. Great and sharp sufferings they may endure, but the Lord sweetens them with answerable consolations, 2 Cor. vii. 4, 'I am filled with comfort, I am exceeding joyful in all our tribulation.' The lowest ebbs are followed with the highest tides; the greatest troubles need not give an interruption to their peace."[8]

---

6. Flavel, *England's Duty*, 4:226.
7. Flavel, *England's Duty*, 4:227.
8. Flavel, *England's Duty*, 4:227.

You can have peace despite troubles. You can have joy despite weeping. Why? Because if you're saved, you have Christ! And Christ, ultimately, is the richest treasure any could ever hope to find, infinitely sweeter than any would dare to imagine, and His delights never end.

Oh, afflicted and weary saint, if your weeping is tarrying along with you, and your spiritual depression has no end, then calamity has called you to take up your arms and do battle. We begin the battle, then, by doing the following.

Remember the Grace of God

This may seem a simple thing to do, but what a grand inner revival it may work at just the right time. The apostle Paul, in considering the grace of God, wrote to the church at Ephesus, "Unto me, who am less than the least of all saints, is this grace given, that I should preach among the Gentiles the unsearchable riches of Christ" (Eph. 3:8). Even we who are least of the saints have been lavished with the perfect love and grace of God through Christ. It is this grace that we live by, and this grace we proclaim to others. At the same time, this grace contains within itself the unsearchable riches of Christ.

Because of grace, we have the richness of being united to Christ, our King. Richard Sibbes beautifully wrote,

> The excellency of this condition to be one with Christ, is, that all things are ours. For he is the King, and the church the Queen of all. All things are serviceable to us. It is a wondrous nearness, to be nearer to Christ, than the angels, who are not his body, but servants that attend upon the church. The bride is nearer to him than the angels, for, "he is the head and husband thereof, and not of the angels," Heb. 2:16. What an excellent condition is this for poor flesh and blood, that creeps up and down the earth here despised![9]

Christ, our King, is ours! This thought alone ought to lift the soul from the pits of despair and into the heavenly realms of rejoicing!

---

9. Richard Sibbes, *Bowels Opened: Being Expository Sermons on Cant. IV. 16, V., VI.*, in *Works of Richard Sibbes*, ed. Alexander B. Grosart (Edinburgh: Banner of Truth, 1983), 2:26.

And, as Sibbes would go on to say, this is all of God's grace, and not at all any of our own doing: "What hope there is to have him, whenas he sueth to us by his messengers, and wooeth us, whenas we should rather seek to him; and with other messengers sendeth a privy messenger, his Holy Spirit, to incline our hearts. Let us therefore, as we love our souls, suffer ourselves to be won."[10]

While we were strangers, foreigners, and enemies of the kingdom of God, the Father and the Son sent forth the Holy Spirit as a beloved messenger to draw, woo, and win us to Christ. *This* is amazing grace, and it is ours!

When you are downcast you must consider not only the unsearchable riches found in Christ; consider Christ Himself.

Remember the Work of Jesus
Set your eyes on Christ and remember how He waded through the darkest of nights and fiercest of storms. Robert Trail, in a sermon on Ephesians 3:8, considered the mediatory work of Jesus and concluded that His willingness to endure affliction was predicated on His fervent love for us:

> Nothing constrained him: he was absolutely free. If his own love in a manner constrained him, the more lovely and excellent is he. What happiness wanted he? What can be added to him? If all men had perished, he had lost nothing. But indeed, when he hath taken on him the work of saving his own, none of them can perish. Had he such a desire to have a company of sinful men and women to be with him for ever? Who can sufficiently admire it? our misery calls for this riches of grace and mercy....
>
> If the redemption of all the elect had cost him but one petition or word to justice, it had been matchless love to have bestowed it. But when it was required that he should be a man, and such a man,—and lead such a life, and die such a death,—to be accused by the law, deserted of his Father and of all creatures, and to have Satan and the world let loose upon him,—oh, what love is here, and how great riches and excellency![11]

---

10. Sibbes, *Bowels Opened*, 2:27.
11. Robert Trail, *Select Practical Writings* (Edinburgh: Banner of Truth, 2020), 208.

If it was His love for us that caused Jesus to endure with patience and hope all the many trials of His earthly life, surely, in love for Him, we can wait and hope with much patience and endurance. Surely, out of love for Him, we can fight against the soul's dark night. Surely, in love, we can follow Christ's example.

Remember too, even when you fall short of Christ's example, that He upholds you in the storm just as He did Peter on the waters (Matt. 14:22–33). But as you do so, also make sure you are prepared for the battle.

There be dragons ahead.

Remember to Wear Your Armor
A prerequisite for entering battle is to have the right mindset and the right armor. By focusing on both grace and Jesus, we will have the right mindset. But what of our armor? Ephesians 6:10–18 lays it out for us:

> Finally, my brethren, be strong in the Lord, and in the power of his might. Put on the whole armour of God, that ye may be able to stand against the wiles of the devil. For we wrestle not against flesh and blood, but against principalities, against powers, against the rulers of the darkness of this world, against spiritual wickedness in high places. Wherefore take unto you the whole armour of God, that ye may be able to withstand in the evil day, and having done all, to stand. Stand therefore, having your loins girt about with truth, and having on the breastplate of righteousness; and your feet shod with the preparation of the gospel of peace; above all, taking the shield of faith, wherewith ye shall be able to quench all the fiery darts of the wicked. And take the helmet of salvation, and the sword of the Spirit, which is the word of God: praying always with all prayer and supplication in the Spirit, and watching thereunto with all perseverance and supplication for all saints.

Since our battle is far more spiritual than physical, neither camouflage nor chain mail will be of any help to you. We need to wear the spiritual armor that God has prepared for us. Apart from it, we will not stand against the schemes of Satan. Without it, we will be overcome by the dark night of the soul.

Though all the pieces are essential and vital, when it comes to battling spiritual depression, perhaps the most important piece of our body to dress is the feet, since God has offered to shod our feet with the gospel of peace itself. While we certainly need to gird ourselves with truth so that we can defeat the lies of Satan and the lies of self, it is the gospel—and the comfort that comes through it—that will be of the greatest help.

William Gurnall, author of that wonderful *The Christian in Complete Armour*, has some words of advice for you, quoted at length here:

> The great question I expect now to fall from thy mouth, Christian, is not how mayst thou escape these troubles and trials which, as the evil genius of the gospel, do always attend it? but rather, how thou mayst get this shoe on, thy heart ready for a march to go and meet them when they come, and cheerfully wade through them, whatever they be, or how long soever they stay with thee? This is a question well becoming a Christian soldier, to ask for armour wherewith he may fight; whereas the coward throws away his armour, and asks whether he may flee. I shall therefore give the best counsel I can, in these few particulars.
>
> First Direction. Look carefully to the ground of thy active obedience, that it be sound and sincere.... The same right principles whereby the sincere soul acts for Christ, will carry him to suffer for Christ....
>
> Second Direction. Pray for a suffering spirit. This is not a common gift, which every carnal gospeller and slighty professor hath. No; it is a peculiar gift, and bestowed on a few sincere souls. "Unto you it is given in the behalf of Christ, not only to believe on him, but also to suffer for his sake," Php. 1:29....
>
> Third Direction. Be much in the meditation of a suffering state. He will say his lesson best, when his master calls him forth, that is oftenest conning it over beforehand to himself. Do by the troubles thou mayest meet with, as porters used to do with their burdens—they will lift them again and again, before they take them on their back. Thus do thou. Be often lifting up

in thy meditations those evils that may befall thee for Christ and his truth; and try how thou couldst fadge [agree] with them, if called to endure them....

Fourth Direction. Make a daily resignation of thyself up to the will of God. Indeed this should be, as it were, the lock of the night and the key of the morning. We should open and shut our eyes with this recommending of ourselves into the hands of God....

Fifth Direction. Make self-denial appear as rational and reasonable as thou canst to thy soul. The stronger the understanding is able to reason for the equity and rationality of any work or duty, the more readily and cheerfully it is done, if the heart is honest and sincere....

Sixth Direction. Labour to carry on the work of mortification every day to further degrees than other. It is the sap in the wood that makes it hard to burn, and corruption unmortified that makes the Christian loath to suffer.... The apostle speaks of some that were "tortured, not accepting deliverance; that they might obtain a better resurrection," Heb. 11:35. They did not like the world so well, as being so far on their journey to heaven—though in hard way—to be willing to come back to live in it any longer.[12]

What Gurnall lays out here is worth meditating on. We must not only think that the battle awaits us when the dark night of the soul visits us but must recognize that it is our duty to constantly be on guard and watch. We must be men and women who will follow Christ, our Captain, into war.

Waiting and Hoping through Spiritual Depression

Spiritual depression is not easy. It can be incredibly trying. Many times, it may beat us down so far that we simply feel like giving up. But we must not. We must, by the grace of God, rush to the battle. We must remember grace, remember Christ, and remember our armor.

---

12. William Gurnall, *The Christian in Complete Armour* (repr., Peabody, Mass.: Hendrickson, 2016), 575–79.

We must be people of prayer who, with eyes resolutely set on Christ and hearts steadfastly submitted to His will, do all for His glory rather than our own. This is where joy is found. We cannot seek to live for our own glory. We cannot permit such sin within our hearts for even a moment. In fact, mortifying sin is so important that Gurnall compares unmortified sin to a tiny rock that sinks a boat:

> Take heed, Christian, of leaving any worldly lust unmortified in thy soul. This will never consent thou shouldest endure much for Christ. Few ships sink at sea; they are the rocks and shelves that split them. Couldst thou get off the rocks of pride and unbelief, and escape knocking on the sands of fear of man, love of the world, thou wouldst do well enough in the greatest storm that can overtake thee in the sea of this world.[13]

Remember that sin may very well be the cause of the spiritual depression. You must not allow it to take root within your soul. Rather, you must fight it with violent tenacity! Do not allow a mere pebble to sink the ship you sail.

It is true that each of us will, on occasion, wade through the dark night of the soul. But spiritual depression does not need to define us.

Edmund Calamy was an English Puritan who was, like so many others, one of those ministers forced from his pulpit during the Great Ejection of 1662. This was truly a dark night of the soul, and he could have allowed it to define himself, giving into depression and despondency. Instead, he prayed. Below you will find one of his prayers from this period of his life, which I pray will help us to overcome our own spiritual depression:

> Oh most Holy, thou ever blessed Lord God, thou fillest heaven and earth with thy presence. We pray thee fill all our hearts with the presence of thy grace, and let it appear that thou art in the midst of us, with that powerful assistance of thy Spirit, that we may receive a token of love from thee at this time....
>
> We confess we have forfeited all our mercies; we have heard much of God, Christ and heaven with our ears, but there is little

---

13. Gurnall, *Christian in Complete Armour*, 579–80.

of God, Christ and heaven in our hearts. We confess, many of us by hearing sermons, are grown sermon-proof; we know how to scoff and mock at sermons, but we know not how to live sermons....

We pray thee that thou wilt glorify thy sovereignty, in being gracious to us, and pardon our many and great transgressions.

Thou makest use of the malice of men for thy glory; thou killest Goliath with his own sword. Oh, help us to put our trust in thee, thou that canst kill, and cure by killing.[14] Amen.

Study Questions

1. What is spiritual depression? Have you ever encountered it before?

2. In what ways is the gospel at stake when it comes to matters of spiritual depression?

3. The communion of the saints is essential in the battle against spiritual depression. Why do we need the help and aid of other Christians?

4. Within the battle plan to fight spiritual depression, which step seems the most difficult? How can you ably practice it the next time you are in the battle yourself?

5. Weeping may tarry for the night. To borrow Gurnall's phrase, how are we to make sure that our boats do not sink from these pebbles?

---

14. Edmund Calamy, "Prayer at Aldermanbury," in *Sermons of the Great Ejection* (Edinburgh: Banner of Truth, 1962), 5–6.

Chapter 10

Joy Comes in the Morning

Weeping will not last. The dark night of the soul will come to an end. Spiritual depression will not define your walk with Christ for eternity. After all, spiritual depression is not a fruit of the spirit. Joy, however, is.

Joy will, ultimately, become the mark of every Christian in glory. While I may not be able to tell you *when* your spiritual depression will come to an end, I can assure you that weeping will end, and joy *will* come. It must. Galatians 5:22–25 lists joy as one of the distinguishing marks of the Christian: "But the fruit of the Spirit is love, joy, peace, longsuffering, gentleness, goodness, faith, meekness, temperance: against such there is no law. And they that are Christ's have crucified the flesh with the affections and lusts. If we live in the Spirit, let us also walk in the Spirit."

Beloved, when you feel as though the weight of despair may finally crush you, remember your Savior, your salvation, and your security. Take no thought for your own unworthiness, because Christ has made you worthy to share in His inheritance. He has qualified you. No saint has ever been worthy on his own to stand before God; an alien righteousness has always been required. Nehemiah Coxe wrote about this exact thing when he examined the covenant of grace that God made with Abraham: "Abraham was not a person eminent for holiness and religion. When God called him to inherit Shem's blessing, he was not better or more deserving than any of the rest of his posterity. Instead, he was swimming down the stream of a wicked world, having degenerated from the religion and piety of his ancestors to false worship and idolatry (Joshua 24:2, 3)."[1]

Could any look to Abraham before God called him and say, "That man, right there, is worthy of the Lord's blessing"? Of course not! Every man, woman, and child whom God has ever called to Himself has been a sinner, completely unworthy of His grace. That's exactly what makes God's sovereign grace so very amazing.

Thomas Watson, in his wonderful treatise on God's sovereignty, *All Things for Good*, wrote,

> When God calls a man by His grace, he cannot but come. You may resist the minister's call, but you cannot the Spirit's call. The finger of the blessed Spirit can write upon a heart of stone, as once He wrote His law upon tables of stone. God's words are creating words; when He says, "Let there be light," there was light, and when He says, "Let there be faith," it shall be so. When God called Paul, he answered to the call. "I was not disobedient to the heavenly vision" (Acts 26:19). God rides forth conquering in the chariot of His gospel; He makes the blind eyes see, and the stony heart bleed. If God will call a man, nothing shall lie in the way to hinder; difficulties shall be united, the powers of hell shall disband. "Who hath resisted his will?" (Rom. 9:19). God bends the iron sinew, and cuts asunder the gates of brass (Psalm 107:6). When the Lord touches a man's heart by His Spirit, all proud imaginations are brought down, and the fort-royal of the will yields to God.[2]

When God regenerates us and makes us willing to come to Him, everything changes. Being imbued with God's life in the soul *must* produce a profound happiness and joy, for God is most happy and most joyful.

---

1. Nehemiah Coxe and John Owen, *Covenant Theology: From Adam to Christ*, ed. Ronald D. Miller, James M. Renihan, and Francisco Orozco (Palmdale, Calif.: Reformed Baptist Academic Press, 2005), Kindle edition, loc. 1106.

2. Thomas Watson, *All Things for Good* (West Linn, Ore.: Monergism Books, 2020), 92.

Putting Joy in Perspective with the Puritans

Some reading this right now may feel slightly estranged from joy, as though it were some foreign thing to be avoided. Perhaps some have even made the categorical error of believing that suffering is necessary for the Christian to endure so that they would mature in the faith, and that maturity in a believer looks a lot like a dour, humdrum, and cynical existence. But that could not be further from the truth. Nearly every Puritan and every Christian that we have looked at in the pages of this book has experienced profound joys, despite trials and suffering. This same joy can, and should, mark us as well.

However, we must be careful to find joy in the *right* things. We must take delight only in those things that are good, lovely, admirable, and worthy of praise. In short, we must make sure we take delight and find joy in God primarily and in the blessings He brings to us secondarily. Primarily, we delight and find joy in God because He is unchanging, but we can secondarily take delight and joy in His blessings to us because *He has chosen to give them to us*. What parent doesn't take pleasure in the delight and joy of their children over themselves and the gifts they give? So God assuredly takes pleasure in our delight and joy in Him and the blessings He gives.

Christopher Love wrote about having the right perspective on joy in *A Christian Directory*. Under a section titled "Immoderate Joy for Worldly Comforts," he encouraged Christians to recognize the following truths about joy:

> Though Christians must take heed that they are not immoderate in their joy for worldly comforts, yet you must know that you are allowed by God to rejoice in the outward comforts that He gives you here in this world. Solomon says, "There is a time to mourn, and a time to laugh" (Ecclesiastes 3:4). And, "Go thy way, eat thy bread with joy, and drink thy wine with a merry heart, live joyfully with the wife whom thou lovest" (Ecclesiastes 9:7, 9). So, "In the day of prosperity be joyful" (Ecclesiastes 7:14). And, "Ye shall rejoice in all that you put your hand unto" (Deuteronomy 12:7). This conclusion is necessary for sad and melancholy Christians who, though they enjoy an affluence

and confluence of worldly comforts, yet will not at all rejoice in them. Beloved, God allows you to rejoice.[3]

Frankly, God does not merely *permit* us to rejoice in His blessings toward us; He expects us to rejoice! This is why the Holy Spirit led Paul to encourage the saints, in Philippians 4:4, to "rejoice in the Lord always: and again I say, Rejoice." God provides us with bountiful blessings in our salvation so that we would rejoice. For this same reason, the psalmist writes that we must "taste and see that the LORD is good: blessed is the man that trusteth in him" (Ps. 34:8) and also says, "Thou hast put gladness in my heart, more than in the time that their corn and their wine increased" (Ps. 4:7). God provides us with a plethora of reasons to rejoice!

So, if you must, begin to count your blessings! In fact, because you must rejoice and praise God, count your blessings! It is not wrong to find joy in these things; it is good and right to rejoice in the God who has supplied all your needs in Christ (Phil. 4:19) and done exceedingly more than we could ever have imagined asking for (Eph. 3:20). So, Love continues: "Consider that religion does not extirpate or annihilate worldly rejoicing, but only regulates it. It is not like a weeding hook to pluck up your joy by the roots, but like a pruning hook to lop off the luxuriancy of it, and to keep your joy in its due decorum.... Beloved, religion does not annihilate, but regulates your joys; nay, being religious rather increases than in any way diminishes your joys."[4]

Did you get that? Christianity *increases* our joys! That is how we know that though weeping tarries for a night, yet joy will still come in the morning. If you are waiting right now for the dark clouds of spiritual depression to lift, take heart, Christian soldier! The battle is not yet over, but Christ has already won the war. Your future joy is a

---

3. Christopher Love, "Directions Concerning Immoderate Joy for Worldly Comforts," A Puritan's Mind, accessed December 2, 2023, https://www.apuritansmind.com/puritan-favorites/christopher-love/directions-concerning-immoderate-joy-for-worldly-comforts/.

4. Love, "Directions Concerning Immoderate Joy."

certainty, so stand firm and fight for it! Take seriously Love's concluding thoughts on the matter:

> Take this conclusion: the worldly joy of a godly man is oftentimes mingled with more inward gripes and grief of spirit than the worldly joy of a wicked man is. As in, "Even in laughter the heart is sorrowful" (Proverbs 14:13). In 2 Corinthians, the apostle there speaks of some who gloried in appearance, but not in heart (2 Corinthians 5:12). The joy of the wicked is but in appearance, not in reality. When they are in their greatest jollity and mirth, even then they have some inward gripes and anguish of conscience that galls and troubles them. A wicked man's joy is like a godly man's sorrow. The former's joy is but in appearance, not in truth. A godly man has something like sorrow, but it is not so indeed; they are but "as sorrowful, yet always rejoicing" (2 Corinthians 6:10). "The blessing of the Lord maketh rich, and He addeth no sorrow with it" (Proverbs 10:22).[5]

The wicked man is never truly joyful. But not so the righteous man. The righteous man is altogether a different story. Though he may suffer great trials and tribulations, yet he may remain forever rejoicing, even in sorrow! That's one of the great benefits of knowing Christ and being known by Him.

Union with Christ Produces Joy in the Saint
Christopher Love was right to encourage Christians to rejoice. But our rejoicing is not dependent on the blessings that God either gives or withholds. Salvation is designed, in part, to bring about rejoicing and praise in God's people. As Isaiah wrote,

> I will greatly rejoice in the LORD, my soul shall be joyful in my God; for he hath clothed me with the garments of salvation, he hath covered me with the robe of righteousness, as a bridegroom decketh himself with ornaments, and as a bride adorneth herself with her jewels. For as the earth bringeth forth her bud, and as the garden causeth the things that are sown in it to spring

---

5. Love, "Directions Concerning Immoderate Joy."

forth; so the Lord GOD will cause righteousness and praise to spring forth before all the nations. (61:10–11)

Being clothed by the righteousness of Christ and having our sin imputed to Him (2 Cor. 5:21) is the basis of both our right standing before God and our rejoicing in Him. Simultaneously, this is the means of our being united to Christ by faith. In fact, our spiritual union with Christ, which is founded on the finished work of His sovereign grace, is the means of a great deal of joy and happiness. John Newton, that great hymn writer, once penned a letter wherein he exalted the wonderful privileges of the Christian's union with Christ. He wrote,

> The union of a believer with Christ is so intimate, so unalterable, so rich in privilege, so powerful in influence, that it cannot be fully represented by any description or similitude taken from earthly things. The mind, like the sight, is incapable of apprehending a great object, without viewing it on different sides. To help our weakness, the nature of this union is illustrated in the Scripture, by four comparisons, each throwing additional light on the subject, yet falling short of the thing signified.[6]

Newton then goes on to explain these four illustrations. First, because we are often tossed to and fro by the trials of this world, Christ has become our sure foundation. Second, because we are born in sin and are by nature separated from God, we are unfruitful; yet we are united to Christ, who is the true and living Vine. Third, we are wicked before the eyes of God, full of all manner of sin toward God and others, yet Christ has become for us our Head, through whom we are righteous, holy, and loving toward God and our fellow man. Finally, Newton notes that we were "naked and destitute, without pity, and without help,"[7] yet Christ has become our Husband and thus we are clothed with His robes, provided for by His riches, and forever given His help and aid. Thus, Newton rightfully concludes his letter by writing,

---

6. John Newton, *Letter XXVIII*, in *The Works of John Newton* (Edinburgh: Banner of Truth, 2015), 1:226–27.

7. Newton, *Letter XXVIII*, 1:227.

> Well may we say, What hath God wrought! How inviolable is the security, how inestimable the privilege, how inexpressible the happiness, of a believer! How greatly is he indebted to grace! He was once afar off, but he is brought nigh to God by the blood of Christ: he was once a child of wrath, but is now an heir of everlasting life. How strong then are his obligations to walk worthy of God, who has called him to his kingdom and glory![8]

Since God has wrought an incredible salvation within us, with a most perfect security and inestimable privilege, our joy and happiness truly does become inexpressible. As Paul reflected on these gospel gifts, he was led to exclaim, "Thanks be unto God for his unspeakable gift" (2 Cor. 9:15). This doesn't mean that we don't know anything about the gift of salvation we have in Christ. It does mean that, when we really start to reflect on our salvation and union with Christ, our joy suddenly becomes so large and great and infinite that expressing it becomes impossible. Our thanksgiving is expressed through words, but the words themselves hardly seem sufficient. Thus, we can say that both the gift of God and the joy in our souls are indescribable.

Indescribable though it may be, our union with Christ is the basis for living life for Christ with joy. As many have said before, we are to live all of life for Christ, knowing we have been given the whole Christ for this life. We don't have a partial Christ, or a piece of Christ, but the *whole* Christ. He's not like a Scrooge, stingily giving only tiny pieces of Himself but reserving the better part for Himself alone. He is the God who lavished us with "wisdom and prudence; having made known unto us the mystery of his will, according to his good pleasure which he hath purposed in himself" (Eph. 1:8–9). He is a God who freely and greatly gives of Himself to His people.

This understanding of union with Christ and His lavishing infinite riches on us produces an unending joy. This is a joy that extends to all of life, in all of its spheres; even our work life is impacted. We can work for the glory of God with joy in our hearts, knowing that

---

8. Newton, *Letter XXVIII*, 1:227–28.

whether we are bakers, construction workers, painters, electricians, or pastors, all our work has eternal significance and value. Consider, as Joel Beeke explained, the Puritan vision of work and vocation:

> The Puritans believed that only the God-fearer:
>
> - Enjoys his work not just as a job that provides the necessities of life, but as a calling from God. Fearing God, he enjoys every aspect of his work and relishes every accomplishment as a token of God's love and grace.
>
> - Works with a God-glorifying purpose in view. This basic integrity preserves him from much trouble; it enables him to transact all his business with scriptural integrity, diligence, and zeal. It helps him pursue his goals with zeal.
>
> - Trusts in God's promise of provision. Like the widow of Zarephath, he trusts that God will provide even if his supplies dwindle.
>
> - Handles life's disappointments with spiritual maturity, resting by faith in the sovereign purposes of God.
>
> - Knows that he will enjoy for eternity God's gracious reward upon his good work and his good works.
>
> Consequently, the Puritan view of secular work is theologically rich.[9]

We must grasp this truth: the whole Christ has been given to us. We have not only His body but His blood as well, which is symbolized in the Lord's Supper of bread and wine. It is His body that nourishes us, His blood that sustains us, His whole self that purifies, cleanses, and sanctifies us. If we are truly united to this Christ, then joy must come in the morning!

Fighting for Joy with the Puritans
How do we fight for joy in the morning? With the help of the

---

9. Joel R. Beeke, "5 Reasons the Puritans Were So Joyful," March 30, 2019, The Gospel Coalition, https://www.thegospelcoalition.org/article/5-reasons-puritans-joyful/.

Puritans, we will see how the battle for joy is won through faith, patience, and hope.

Faith in the Truth Is Both the Main Defense and the Main Weapon in Our Battle for Joy

When we examined the armor of God in Ephesians 6 with the help of William Gurnall, we noted how very important it is to protect the spiritual feet so that we do not fall in battle. But just as urgently as we need our feet shod with the gospel of peace, we also need the shield of faith and the sword of truth. Used in tandem, faith defends us from the schemes of the evil one and truth puts us on the assault.

What is the truth we wield? The Bible. Where is our faith placed? In the truth of the Bible, especially as it reveals the person, nature, and work of Jesus Christ. Faith in Christ, then, acts as a defense against sorrow and spiritual depression while also emboldening us to tear down strongholds of doubt and discouragement. This is not "name it and claim it" theology but rather practical theology. This is, effectively, "believe it and apply it."

Jesus, then, becomes both our Defender and Protector as He defends us from the enemy and leads us to assail the gates of hell. This becomes clear as we consider how we fight for joy and rejoice in the goodness of God despite spiritual depression.

The dilemma of spiritual depression and the need for joy is laid out in Psalm 42:11: "Why art thou cast down, O my soul? and why art thou disquieted within me? hope thou in God: for I shall yet praise him, who is the health of my countenance, and my God." William Bridge's *A Lifting Up for the Downcast* speaks to all of this and more, especially in his recorded sermon, "The Cure of Discouragement by Faith in Jesus Christ." Bridge offered the following help: "You have heard of the saints' discouragements, and the unreasonableness of them; there is no just cause or reason for their discouragements. Would you now hear of some means against them? The Psalmist saith in these words, 'Hope thou in God,' or trust thou in God, or wait thou on God. And so the doctrine plainly is this: Faith is the help against all discouragements."[10]

By this, Bridge did not mean to suggest that there is never a reason for our discouragement. On the contrary, as the preceding pages of this book will attest, there are often a plethora of reasons for our discouragements and spiritual depression. However, in light of Christ and eternity, all our afflictions will appear quite dim and small. The key to victory in this spiritual battle for joy is, primarily, faith in Christ.

Hoping, Trusting, and Waiting on God Are the Expressions of Faith That Bring Us Victory
As we have seen from the start of this book, waiting through trials and hoping in God are the keys to experiencing the Puritan hope of triumph through suffering. They are also the outward expressions of our faith in Jesus and ultimately the tools used to bring us joy. Indeed, Bridge concurred with this sentiment by explaining that "hoping, trusting, waiting on God, is the special, if not the only means appointed against all discouragements. 'I had verily fainted, unless I had believed, (saith David,) to see the goodness of the Lord in the land of the living.' I had fainted, unless I had believed. Faith bears up the heart against all discouragements."[11]

A Patient Reliance on God Will Bring Us Victory in Our Battle for Joy
We see that our faith in Jesus is a defense against our enemies and a weapon in our hands to assault those monuments of sorrow and spiritual depression. Used rightly, faith really can bring us joy as it reminds us of all the promises of God that find their "yea" and "Amen" in Jesus (2 Cor. 1:20).

But when we have faith in Jesus to wait and hope, there is one more piece of the puzzle that is essential, and that is patient reliance. We live in an age where we want things *immediately*. Most foods have microwavable options for this very reason—we live at such a

---

10. William Bridge, *A Lifting Up for the Downcast* (West Linn, Ore.: Monergism Books, 2021), 268.

11. Bridge, *Lifting Up for the Downcast*, 269.

blisteringly fast pace; we do not know how to slow down and wait *patiently*. We want to take things into our own hands and make them happen *now*.

Patient reliance, however, teaches and reminds us that we can do nothing on our own. We need the Lord. As God said to Moses and the Israelites in Exodus 14:14, "The LORD shall fight for you, and ye shall hold your peace." The Israelites spent an entire night near the Red Sea, anxiously wondering how God would bring them victory over Pharoah and his army. But in the morning, they saw the Red Sea had parted, and God led them across on dry ground. We must learn the truth that we can do nothing apart from God and that, without Him, victory is impossible. Yet He is working for us. He is defending us and fighting for us. Like the Israelites, we must wait and hope with a patient reliance, faithfully trusting what God is doing on our behalf—even when we cannot see His working for ourselves.

Our waiting and hoping will never be done faithfully or joyfully if we do not know how to wait and hope patiently. Again, Bridge wrote, "To hope in God, is to expect help from God; to trust in God, is to rely or rest upon God for help; and to wait on him, is to continue and abide in this expectation or reliance. Properly, according to scripture phrase, trusting in God is the recumbency or the reliance of the soul upon God in Christ, for some good thing that lies out of sight."[12]

There would be no need for patiently waiting and hoping if we saw the end from the beginning, but only God has such foreknowledge and foresight. Our task, beloved, is to faithfully—and patiently—wait and hope on the Lord to bring us everlasting joy.

Waiting at Night and Hoping for Joy in the Morning

Wait and hope. These two words really do summarize much of the Christian life, do they not? No matter the trial we discuss, these words will apply.

When the dark night of the soul comes and we are waiting, sometimes with bated breath and exhausted patience, for joy to come anew in the morning, it can feel an eternity. Yet it is often the case that in

---

12. Bridge, *Lifting Up for the Downcast*, 269.

such instances of waiting and hoping, we are rather surprised to find that joy has suddenly come to us in the most extraordinary of ways.

While looking to Christ is important here, there may be no greater way to combat spiritual depression than with God's Word. We need to utilize the Scriptures by studying and mediating on them. We need to apply them to our lives and live by them. But during combat against spiritual depression, should it be so strange to find joy and mirth swelling in our hearts? Surely, as we gaze up at Christ in His glory through His Word, our downcast hearts must soon begin to lift in joyful adoration. And joyful adoration needs an outlet—like the song of the angels announcing the birth of Christ in Luke 2:14—to express itself.

Thus, the Puritans recognized song as a proper channel of both praising God and lifting hearts. In the preface to a Psalter from 1650, Puritans like John Owen, Thomas Manton, Thomas Watson, and many others wrote,

> The promises of God's holy covenant, which are to others as stale news or withered flowers, feed the pleasure of their minds; and the mysteries of our redemption by Christ are their hearts' delight and comfort. But as joy must have a proper object, so also a vent: for this is an affection that cannot be penned up: the usual issue and out-going of it is by singing. Profane spirits must have songs suitable to their mirth; as their mirth is carnal, so their songs are vain and frothy, if not filthy and obscene; but they that rejoice in the Lord, their mirth runneth in a spiritual channel: "Is any merry? let him sing psalms," saith the apostle (Jas. 5:13); and, "Thy statutes have been my songs in the house of my pilgrimage," saith holy David (Ps. 119:54).[13]

If the singing of psalms is an avenue for expressing joy, then it should be little surprise that singing is itself a way to lift the heart. And as we think on our union with Christ, all the riches lavished on us by God in our salvation, and the many promises we have in God's Word—the heart ought to radiate with songs of mirth, joy, and praise unto the Lord!

---

13. "Puritan Preface to the 1650 Psalter," The 1650 Psalter, accessed December 2, 2023, https://1650psalter.com/puritan-preface-to-the-1650-psalter/.

Poetry, like song, can also have the same effect. Many of the Puritans have a poetic quality to their writings, and some, like John Bunyan, wrote a great deal of verse. But when it comes to poems that lift the heart and explain the value of song in the life of the Christian, the work of John Masefield quickly comes to mind.

Truth be told, John Masefield is decidedly not a Puritan—far from it. But he is one of my favorite poets. He was born toward the end of the nineteenth century and lived well into the 1960s. He was also the British Poet Laureate from 1930 to 1967, having the title bestowed on him by the appointment of King George V by way of recommendation by Prime Minister Ramsay MacDonald.

If Masefield understood one thing well, it was the need to fight our battles with joy and mirth. For this reason, I turn your attention to his poem "Laugh and Be Merry":

> Laugh and be merry, remember, better the world with a song,
> Better the world with a blow in the teeth of a wrong.
> Laugh, for the time is brief, a thread the length of a span.
> Laugh and be proud to belong to the old proud pageant of man.
>
> Laugh and be merry: remember, in olden time.
> God made Heaven and Earth for joy He took in a rhyme,
> Made them, and filled them full with the strong red wine
>   of His mirth
> The splendid joy of the stars: the joy of the earth.
>
> So we must laugh and drink from the deep blue cup of the sky,
> Join the jubilant song of the great stars sweeping by,
> Laugh, and battle, and work, and drink of the wine outpoured
> In the dear green earth, the sign of the joy of the Lord.
>
> Laugh and be merry together, like brothers akin,
> Guesting awhile in the rooms of a beautiful inn,
> Glad till the dancing stops, and the lilt of the music ends.
> Laugh till the game is played; and be you merry, my friends.[14]

---

14. John Masefield, "Laugh and Be Merry," in *Poems: Complete Edition with Recent Poems* (New York: Macmillan, 1974), 51–52.

Let us take these words to heart. Let us laugh and let us be merry, for our Lord is faithful and true, and He is King. There is no news more glorious, or joy stirring, than this.

As we rejoice, we ought to seek others to rejoice with. But solitude is no reason to quit our rejoicing either. The one who quits rejoicing is much more liable to experience the dark night of the soul. So, rejoice in the Lord always, and again I say, rejoice (Phil. 4:4)!

True, it may feel as though we suffer alone at times and as though the morning may never come. Our deepest sorrows, greatest trials, and most wonderful triumphs may go mostly unnoticed by others in this world. No matter. We still live before Christ and for Him. Whether before hundreds or none, let us remember we live for an audience of one. Whether we live or die, we do all for the glory of God alone.

As things stand in this world, sin surrounds us and trials rage. This is not how it will always be, though. Deep down, we know this, and we long for the future day when our faith will be made sight, our bodies will be resurrected in glory, and we will reign with Jesus on the new earth for all eternity. Deep down, we know that one day the sun will go down to never rise again, because the Son of God Himself will become our permanent light. In that everlasting *Son*rise, we will have everlasting joy. As we wait and hope with longing for that coming day, let us find solace in the words of Arthur Bennett below:

> O LORD,
>   I live here as a fish in a vessel of water,
>   only enough to keep me alive,
>   but in heaven I shall swim in the ocean.
> Here I have a little air in me to keep me breathing,
>   but there I shall have sweet and fresh gales;
> Here I have a beam of sun to lighten my darkness,
>   a warm ray to keep me from freezing;
>   yonder I shall live in light and warmth for ever.
> My natural desires are corrupt and misguided,
>   and it is thy mercy to destroy them;
> My spiritual longings are of thy planting,
>   and thou wilt water and increase them;

Quicken my hunger and thirst after the realm above.
Here I can have the world,
   there I shall have thee in Christ;
Here is a life of longing and prayer,
   there is assurance without suspicion,
     asking without refusal;
Here are gross comforts, more burden than benefit,
   there is joy without sorrow,
     comfort without suffering,
     love without inconstancy,
     rest without weariness.
Give me to know that heaven is all love,
   where the eye affects the heart,
     and the continual viewing of thy beauty
       keeps the soul in continual transports of delight.
Give me to know that heaven is all peace,
   where error, pride, rebellion, passion raise no head.
Give me to know that heaven is all joy,
   the end of believing, fasting, praying,
   mourning, humbling, watching, fearing, repining;
And lead me to it soon.[15] Amen.

---

15. Arthur Bennett, "Earth and Heaven," in *The Valley of Vision* (Edinburgh: Banner of Truth, 1975), 203.

Study Questions

1. How can we be sure that the dark night of the soul will come to an end and that joy will come in the morning?

2. What does Nehemiah Coxe teach us about our being made worthy to come before God in Christ?

3. Christopher Love wrote about godly joy in *A Christian Directory*. What lessons does he teach us?

4. How is union with Christ a means of joy?

5. As we wait and hope for joy to come in the morning through the Lord, how can we begin *now* to fight for joy?

CONCLUSION

The Puritan Hope of Triumph in the Midst of Suffering

William Carey, remembered today as the father of modern missions, once preached a sermon that, today, is called his "Deathless" sermon. The irony is that the sermon—as far as scholars know—no longer exists in a completed form in any writing. Yet it has taken on the reputation of being one of the most important sermons preached over the past few centuries. While no complete record exists, we do have documentation of what text of Scripture was preached and what Carey's two main points were.

Carey's text was Isaiah 54:2–3: "Enlarge the place of thy tent, and let them stretch forth the curtains of thine habitations: spare not, lengthen thy cords, and strengthen thy stakes; for thou shalt break forth on the right hand and on the left; and thy seed shall inherit the Gentiles, and make the desolate cities to be inhabited." From this text, Carey is believed to have exposited two main points relating to the evangelistic mission of the church: (1) expect great things from God; (2) attempt great things for God.

As we consider the Puritan hope of triumph in suffering, we must remember Carey's two main points, for it all goes together. We who expect great things from God must be willing to attempt great things for God. To experience suffering is no blow against God's promises, and thus our expectations must not change, no matter what is happening around us. We who expect great things from God must see and believe that God is working great things out of trials. Despite suffering, we must continue to attempt great things for God, entrusting the results of our efforts to Him.

As we draw this book to a close, let's consider a few final encouraging thoughts from the Puritans that—I pray—will be of some comfort, assurance, and joy to you as we wait and hope for great things while attempting great things.

Christ's Gospel Victory and the Saints' Enduring Hope
Here's the news to be received with much joy: Christ is victorious! His gospel will spread in every place He has ordained, His elect will be gathered in every place and time He has ordained, His saints will be preserved in every way, and His kingdom will come as His will is done, both on earth and in heaven.

Thomas Goodwin exhorts us to grasp this great truth—this Puritan hope of triumph—for ourselves:

> Hath God singled thee out of a family where never one was converted before? This is thy privilege, thou didst first trust in Christ, and thou art the first-fruits that hast sanctified that family unto God; it is likely he will have more out of it, for you know the first-fruits sanctified the lump. Certainly there is that covenant which God makes with nations, that where he beginneth to convert, there are the first-fruits of more to come; and God goeth on to continue that covenant to that nation for ever, though for a while he may cast them off; for they that are converted are the first-fruits. You may observe it, that scarce ever the gospel came to a nation, but it hath continued more or less to this day. The Christian name is as much over the world as ever it was; though Turks dwell with them, and domineer and tyrannise over them, yet the Christian name is in all nations where it once was, because the first converted were the first-fruits of those nations that sanctified the whole lump. Therefore was Abraham called the Father of the Faithful; he was one of the first great believers in a way of difficulty.[1]

Difficulties *will* come to all people in all places where Christ is named as Lord. The faithful will still suffer. There can be little doubt

---

1. Thomas Goodwin, *An Exposition of the Epistle to the Ephesians*, in *The Works of Thomas Goodwin* (Eureka, Calif.: Tanski Publications, 1996), 1:222.

of this. Yet in every place where Christ is named as Lord and difficulties come, still God preserves His people and continues to build His kingdom.

These eternally enduring truths can comfort us as we are defended from the fiery blasts of Satan and his followers, while also enabling us to go on the offensive with the gospel against the enemies of Christ and His church. In Christ, we have all we need to storm the gates of hell because He has promised that they will not prevail against Christ, His church, or His gospel (Matt. 16:17–19).

Satan is described in Scripture as a prowling lion, seeking whom he may devour (1 Peter 5:8), but the Christian need no longer fear him or his schemes. This is because Jesus came to this earth to disarm Satan and all other wicked principalities and, through His death and resurrection, has openly triumphed over Satan (Col. 2:15). Jesus took on Himself the weak vessel of a man and yet succeeded as the Dragon Slayer (Gen. 3:15). Satan thought he was strong, but Jesus is infinitely stronger still. When Jesus entered this world—the domain of Satan and his kingdom—Jesus humiliated the devil by entering his home, binding him, and then plundering his goods (Matt. 12:29). We, as the elect, are the goods that Jesus is continuing to plunder! We are the riches and spoils of war that Jesus has won! And, now, Jesus sends us forth into a world where Satan is no longer the ferocious, roaring lion he once was. Now, for the Christian, Satan is more like an oversize cat that has effectively been declawed and defanged. Still a nuisance, for sure, and he can cause havoc for the unprepared, but he cannot defeat us or reclaim us as his own. Christ holds us secure and leads us into the battlefield of the world Himself.

When we consider our place in the world, then, we must recognize ourselves as soldiers in Christ's army. Soldiers sometimes suffer, but our Captain is alongside us. When we are weak, He is still strong (2 Cor. 12:10). Though we may suffer and, at times, feel defeated, the war has already been won by Christ. Effectively, Jesus is leading us out onto a battlefield that He has already conquered, and His charge is for us to plunder the spoils of war. This is accomplished through the proclamation of the kingly summons, "Repent ye, and believe the gospel" (Mark 1:15). As Cornelius Van Til rightly noted, "Is it not true that Christianity was meant to conquer the whole world for Christ? Yes it is.... If we can successfully defend the fortress of Christian theism, we have the whole world to ourselves. There is, then, no standing room left for the enemy. We wage offensive as well as defensive warfare. The two cannot be separated. But we need not leave the fort in order to wage offensive warfare."[2]

Yes, trials will come, and the Christian will suffer. But we can go through trials and we can endure suffering with hope as we wait for the fulfillment of the victorious promises that are ours in Christ. We can, effectively, be comforted *while* we battle. This peculiar juxtaposition of enjoying comfort while battling and suffering is the Christian's hope alone. No other religion, no other man, no other *thing* offers what Christ offers the saint in salvation—namely, a promise of ultimate and everlasting victory.

These truths are what compelled John Owen, in a sermon preached before Parliament, to rejoice in the conquest of Christ over the nations. In the same spirit that carried William Carey a century later, Owen boldly proclaimed,

> That God in his appointed time will bring forth the kingdom of the Lord Christ unto more glory and power than in former days, I presume you are persuaded. Whatever will be more, these six things are clearly promised:
>
> 1. Fulness of peace unto the gospel and the professors thereof, Isa. 11.6, 7, 54.13, 33.20, 21; Rev. 21.15.
>
> 2. Purity and beauty of ordinances and gospel worship, Rev. 11.2, 21.3. The tabernacle was wholly made by appointment, Mal. 3.3, 4; Zech. 14.16; Rev. 21.27; Zech. 14.20; Isa. 35.8.
>
> 3. Multitudes of converts, many persons, yea, nations, Isa. 60.7, 8, 66.8, 49.18–2; Rev. 7.9.
>
> 4. The full casting out and rejecting of all will-worship, and their attendant abominations, Rev. 11.2.

---

2. Cornelius Van Til, *Christian Apologetics*, 2nd ed., ed. William Edgar (Phillipsburg, N.J.: P&R Publishing, 2003), 23.

5. Professed subjection of the nations throughout the whole world unto the Lord Christ, Dan. 2.44, 7.26, 27; Isa. 60.6–9;—the kingdoms become the kingdoms of our Lord and his Christ (Rev. 11.15), amongst whom his appearance shall be so glorious, that David himself shall be said to reign.

6. A most glorious and dreadful breaking of all that rise in opposition unto him, Isa. 60.12—never such desolations, Rev. 16.17–9.[3]

Beloved, pondering these great truths should cause us to be bold and courageous in our afflictions as we follow and serve Christ on this earth. Be confident that Christ's gospel and kingdom will prevail.

Of course, one does not need to embrace any particular strand of eschatology to appreciate what Owen was preaching about. The mission of the church was given by Jesus in the Great Commission of Matthew 28:19–20, "Go ye therefore, and teach all nations, baptizing them in the name of the Father, and of the Son, and of the Holy Ghost: teaching them to observe all things whatsoever I have commanded you." This is predicated on two promises, which bookend the Great Commission: "And Jesus came and spake unto them, saying, All power is given unto me in heaven and in earth.... And lo, I am with you always, even unto the end of the world. Amen." (Matt. 28:18, 20). Because Jesus has all authority and has promised to be with us eternally, we can confidently go forth to make disciples, which is accomplished through the preaching of the gospel, the baptizing of converts in the triune name of God, and the teaching of the full counsel of God's Word (Acts 20:27).

This is the church's Great Commission, and it will be successful because God promised as much in Isaiah 9:7 when He said, "Of the increase of his government and peace there shall be no end, upon the throne of David, and upon his kingdom, to order it, and to establish it with judgment and with justice from henceforth even for ever. The zeal of the LORD of hosts will perform this." Jesus's kingdom will spread across this earth according to the zeal of the Lord of hosts.

---

3. As quoted in Murray, *Puritan Hope*, 38.

God will most certainly keep His Word, which means we merely need to be faithful. We must follow Christ, submit to His will, and obey His Word, but the success is up to God.

What does all of this have to do with our waiting and hoping through suffering? Everything! The fact that we are citizens of the kingdom of heaven means that the spread of the kingdom across the earth through the proclamation of the gospel is a promise that should bring great assurance and comfort. The fact that the discipling of saints will take place throughout the nations should make us rejoice in our King and God. All of this, coupled with the promise of Christ's glory covering the earth as the waters cover the seas (Hab. 2:14), is intrinsically linked with our own joy and happiness. The certainty of Christ being glorified, and His kingdom being built, is the certainty of future glory and perfect joy for us as His saints (Isa. 9:2–3).

Waiting and Hoping for an Eternal Reward
If all of this were not enough, we must also be confident that God will reward genuine righteousness. Matthew 6:4 promises that our Father will reward us for our righteousness, even if no one else does.

Here's some really good news: salvation is not a reward that we must earn; it is a gift that is to be received because it has been earned by Christ. Salvation is not something for which we must work to keep, because it has been secured by Christ. Yet salvation will produce righteous deeds in our lives, and God has promised to openly reward genuine righteousness.

Is it not wondrously good news that our heavenly Father sees all that we do, even when others don't, and will ultimately reward us far beyond anything this world could possibly offer or give? When bosses fail to see our good work and so we miss out on the promotion or raise, our heavenly Father sees and will one day reward us. When we give of our time, effort, strength, and energy to serve the body of Christ, or the poor, or our neighbors, and yet receive no thanks in return, our heavenly Father sees, and He will reward us! When we suffer various trials, tribulations, and sorrows, there is hope of eternal glory that far outweighs all the suffering we experience here! As

2 Corinthians 4:16–18 promises, "For which cause we faint not; but though our outward man perish, yet the inward man is renewed day by day. For our light affliction, which is but for a moment, worketh for us a far more exceeding and eternal weight of glory; while we look not at the things which are seen, but at the things which are not seen: for the things which are seen are temporal; but the things which are not seen are eternal."

As Jesus promised the church at Smyrna, so He promises us, "Fear none of those things which thou shalt suffer: behold, the devil shall cast some of you into prison, that ye may be tried; and ye shall have tribulation ten days: be thou faithful unto death, and I will give thee a crown of life" (Rev. 2:10). We may not be thrown into prison or suffer for ten days exactly, but the principle remains the same: we who are faithful in suffering will be rewarded in glory. Indeed, 1 Peter 5:4 promises that "when the chief Shepherd shall appear, ye shall receive a crown of glory that fadeth not away."

Yet even this unfading crown of glory and all other heavenly rewards will pale in comparison to our glorious King, for when we gaze on Him, we will recognize that Jesus alone is our eternal treasure, which no moth or rust can corrupt and no thief can steal (Matt. 6:19). Recognizing this glorious and eternal reality will cause us to do just what Revelation 4:10–11 has promised we will do: "The four and twenty elders fall down before him that sat on the throne, and worship him that liveth for ever and ever, and cast their crowns before the throne, saying, Thou art worthy, O Lord, to receive glory and honour and power: for thou hast created all things, and for thy pleasure they are and were created."

We will one day cast our crowns before Jesus, for He alone is worthy of such praise. In anticipation of this future reality, we can live now in submission before this most glorious God. Faithfully submitting to God's will and living righteously despite suffering is not something that God has called us to without first leading by example. Jesus Himself suffered immensely but endured it all. Therefore, Philippians 2:5–11 commands,

> Let this mind be in you, which was also in Christ Jesus: who, being in the form of God, thought it not robbery to be equal with God: but made himself of no reputation, and took upon him the form of a servant, and was made in the likeness of men: and being found in fashion as a man, he humbled himself, and became obedient unto death, even the death of the cross. Wherefore God also hath highly exalted him, and given him a name which is above every name: that at the name of Jesus every knee should bow, of things in heaven, and things in earth, and things under the earth; and that every tongue should confess that Jesus Christ is Lord, to the glory of God the Father.

We must be content to follow in the example of our Lord and Savior, knowing that "godliness with contentment is great gain" (1 Tim. 6:6). Our duty, even in suffering, is to exercise a godly contentment that is satisfied with being righteous for God's glory, even when no one else is watching. It is also a godly contentment and satisfaction with being righteous when others are watching so that they glorify God and not you. Remember: God will punish hypocritical and self-seeking righteousness. He will, however, openly reward righteous deeds that seek His glory. Despite what we may suffer, our goal ought always to be to glorify God. Thomas Watson encourages us to do just this with the promise that "Christ is a king to reward his people. There is nothing lost by serving this king. He rewards his subjects in this life. He gives them inward peace and joy; a bunch of grapes by the way; and oft-times riches and honour…. The great reward is to come…. Christ makes all his subjects kings…. This crown will be full of jewels, and it will 'never fade.'"[4]

This was the Puritan hope: That God would bring an end to our suffering, increase our joy, and bring us to where He is, that we might rule eternally alongside Him. This is our hope too.

I trust that the Puritans quoted within these pages have been of some help, comfort, and encouragement to you.

---

4. Thomas Watson, *A Body of Divinity* (Edinburgh: Banner of Truth, 1965; originally printed as *A Body of Practical Divinity*, 1692), 189.

Waiting and Hoping with Purpose

Trials, conflicts, and sufferings are not peculiar to the Christian life only, but these things do take on far greater significance for the follower of Christ. While the one opposed to Christ will also suffer, their trials serve only one purpose, and that is to act as a warning of the judgment and wrath to come from which they are called on to flee and turn to Christ. But for the Christ-follower, the smallest and greatest sufferings alike are designed by God to draw us closer to Christ, to conform us to the image of Christ, and to cause us to bow our knees before Christ. No matter what, we can see the providential care of our sovereign Lord over our lives, whether it be the best or worst of times. No matter what, we can endure our trials by the grace of God, while patiently waiting and earnestly hoping to experience the full extent of the triumphant victory that is ours in Christ.

Trials, conflicts, and sufferings are the graces and mercies of a loving God who utilizes these means to bow our knees before Him, so that we would glory in Him alone and learn to make much of Him only. It is my prayer that the one reading this has already bowed the knee before Christ as their Lord and Savior. But if you haven't, I implore you to look to the fiercest trials you've yet faced and realize that, even if you multiplied your sorrows to infinity, they cannot compare with the suffering that awaits unrepentant sinners in the lake of fire that burns with God's just wrath eternally.

Now, look to Christ and realize that those same sorrows, multiplied to infinity, are nothing compared to the glory that awaits those who repent of their sin and trust in Jesus. For the Christian, there is an eternal weight of glory prepared by God and kept secure for His children.

The Puritans were taught the humble posture of bowing before Jesus, and I pray that, through the trials of this life, you would be taught to bow the knee to Christ. Pray out to Him and submit to Him. If you refuse, one day your knees will be broken by the King, and you will be forcefully bent to bow before Him. At that point, salvation will no longer be possible, but you will still fulfill your purpose and glorify Him in judgment.

Beloved saints, the triumphant hope of Christ is ours. Let us wait and hope for that victory to be poured out on us. Until then, let us endure the trials and labor in Christ's kingdom, knowing our reward will be all the richer in Him.

One way or another, I will see you on your knees before the King.

> Let us pray as our Lord taught us:
> Our Father which art in heaven, hallowed be thy name.
> Thy kingdom come, thy will be done in earth, as it is in heaven.
> Give us this day our daily bread.
> And forgive us our debts, as we forgive our debtors.
> And lead us not into temptation, but deliver us from evil: for thine is the kingdom, and the power, and the glory, for ever. Amen.[5]

Study Questions

1. What is William Carey's famous quote, and how does it speak to our experience of waiting and hoping?

2. Why is the victory of Jesus a source of joy for the Christian?

3. How do the many promises of Scripture shape our outlook on suffering, waiting, and hoping?

4. What is the Puritan hope of triumph, and how does it shape our outlook on suffering, waiting, and hoping?

5. Throughout this book, we have met many Puritans and gleamed from them and their teachings how to endure suffering with hope. Which have been the most helpful? The most trying? Which teachings can you begin, right now, to practice in your own life?

---

5. Matt. 6:9–13.

Bibliography

Adam, Thomas. *Private Thoughts on Religion; Extracted from the Diary of the Rev. Thomas Adam Rector of Wintringham.* London: A. J. Valpy, Red Lion Court, Fleet Street, 1821.

Athanasius. *On the Incarnation.* Translated by a religious of C.S.M.V. S.Th. Louisville, Ky.: GLH Publishing, 2018.

Bayly, Lewis. *The Practice of Piety: Directing a Christian How to Walk, That He May Please God.* Morgan, Pa.: Soli Deo Gloria, 1902.

Beeke, Joel. "5 Reasons the Puritans Were So Joyful," March 30, 2019, The Gospel Coalition. https://www.thegospelcoalition.org/article/5-reasons-puritans-joyful/.

Benge, Dustin, and Nate Pickowicz. *The American Puritans.* Grand Rapids: Reformation Heritage Books, 2020.

Bennett, Arthur. *The Valley of Vision.* Edinburgh: Banner of Truth, 1975.

Bonar, Andrew. *Memoir and Remains of the Rev. Robert Murray M'Cheyne.* 1844. Reprint, Edinburgh: Banner of Truth, 2012.

Bradstreet, Anne. "As Weary Pilgrim, Now at Rest." Poet and Poem, accessed December 2, 2023. https://poetandpoem.com/Anne-Bradstreet/As-weary-pilgrim-now-at-rest.

Bridge, William. *A Lifting Up for the Downcast.* West Linn, Ore.: Monergism Books, 2021.

Brooks, Thomas. *Paradise Opened.* In *The Complete Works of Thomas Brooks.* Vol. 5. Edinburgh: James Nichol, 1867.

———. *Precious Remedies against Satan's Devices*. In *The Works of Thomas Brooks*. Vol. 1. Edited by Alexander B. Grossart. Edinburgh: James Nichol, 1861–67.

Bunyan, John. *Come and Welcome to Jesus Christ: A Plain and Profitable Discourse on John 6:37*. In *The Works of John Bunyan*. Vol. 1. Edinburgh: Banner of Truth, 1991.

———. *Grace Abounding to the Chief of Sinners*. In *The Works of John Bunyan*. Vol. 1. Edinburgh: Banner of Truth, 1991.

Burroughs, Jeremiah. *A Treatise on Earthly-Mindedness*. 1649. Reprint, Grand Rapids: Soli Deo Gloria, 2022.

———. *The Wonders of Jesus*. Crossville, Tenn.: Puritan Publications, 2022.

Butler, Sir William Francis. *Charles George Gordon*. London: Macmillan and Co., 1901.

Calamy, Edmund. "Prayer at Aldermanbury." In *Sermons of the Great Ejection*. Edinburgh: Banner of Truth, 1962.

Calvin, John. *Institutes of the Christian Religion*. Translated by Ford Lewis Battles. Louisville, Ky.: Westminster John Knox Press, 1960.

———. "The True Partaking of the Flesh and Blood of Christ." In *Tracts and Letters*. Vol. 2. Translated Henry Beveridge. Edinburgh: Banner of Truth, 2009.

Collins, Hercules. *An Orthodox Catechism*. Glasgow: Parresia, 2021.

Coxe, Nehemiah, and John Owen. *Covenant Theology: From Adam to Christ*. Edited by Ronald D. Miller, James M. Renihan, and Francisco Orozco. Palmdale, Calif.: Reformed Baptist Academic Press, 2005.

Dallimore, Arnold. *George Whitefield: The Life and Times of the Great Evangelist of the 18th Century Revival*. Vol. 2. Edinburgh: Banner of Truth, 1980.

Donne, John. "Death, Be Not Proud." Poetry Foundation, accessed December 2, 2023. https://www.poetryfoundation.org/poems/44107/holy-sonnets-death-be-not-proud.

———. "Death's Duel." Christian Classics Ethereal Library, accessed December 2, 2023. https://www.ccel.org/ccel/donne/deaths_duel.html.

Dumas, Alexandre. *The Count of Monte Cristo*. Translated by Robin Buss. New York: Penguin Books, 1996.

Durham, James. *The Song of Solomon*. The Geneva Series of Commentaries. Edinburgh: Banner of Truth, 1982.

Edwards, Jonathan. *A History of the Work of Redemption*. Reprint, Edinburgh: Banner of Truth, 2003.

———. "Notes on the Apocalypse." Jonathan Edwards Center at Yale University, accessed December 2, 2023. http://edwards.yale.edu/archive?path=aHR0cDovL2Vkd2FyZHMueWFsZS5lZHUvY2dpLWJpbi9uZXdwaGlsby9nZXRvYmplY3QucGw/Yy40OjQud2plby40NjI3NDIuNDYyNzQ3LjQ2MjcOOS40NjI3NTkuNDYyNzYyLjQ2Mjc2Ng==.

———. "Sinners in the Hands of an Angry God." In *The Works of Jonathan Edwards*. Vol. 2. Edinburgh: Banner of Truth, 1979.

———. "To Sir William Pepperrell." Jonathan Edwards Center at Yale University, accessed December 2, 2023. http://edwards.yale.edu/archive?path=aHR0cDovL2Vkd2FyZHMueWFsZS5lZHUvY2dpLWJpbi9uZXdwaGlsby9nZXRvYmplY3QucGw/Yy4xNToxNy53amVv.

———. "To the Reverend Thomas Gillespie." Jonathan Edwards Center at Yale University, accessed December 2, 2023. http://edwards.yale.edu/archive?path=aHR0cDovL2Vkd2FyZHMueWFsZS5lZHUvY2dpLWJpbi9uZXdwaGlsby9nZXRvYmplY3QucGw/Yy4xNToyMjoxNC53amVv.

Flavel, John. *England's Duty*. In *The Works of John Flavel*. Vol. 4. Reprint, Edinburgh: Banner of Truth, 2021.

———. *The Fountain of Life Opened Up: or, A Display of Christ in His Essential and Mediatorial Glory*. In *The Works of John Flavel*. Vol 1. Reprint, Edinburgh: Banner of Truth, 2021.

Goodwin, Thomas. *An Exposition of the Epistle to the Ephesians*. In *The Works of Thomas Goodwin*. Vol. 1. Eureka, Calif.: Tanski Publications, 1996.

Gurnall, William. *The Christian in Complete Armour*. Reprint, Peabody, Mass.: Hendrickson, 2016.

BIBLIOGRAPHY

Hadaway, Robin A. *A Survey of World Missions.* Nashville, Tenn.: B&H Publishing, 2020.

Hamilton, Ian. *Our Heavenly Shepherd: Comfort and Strength from Psalm 23.* Grand Rapids: Reformation Heritage Books, 2022.

Henry, Matthew. *Matthew Henry's Concise Commentary.* Christian Classics Ethereal Library. Accessed December 2, 2023. https://ccel.org/ccel/henry/mhcc/mhcc.xxxv.xix.html?highlight=John%2019&queryID=30385509&resultID=133298#highlight.

———. *A Method for Prayer: Freedom in the Face of God.* Fearn, Scotland: Christian Heritage, 1994.

Holland, Josiah Gilbert. *Garnered Sheaves: The Complete Poetical Works.* New York: Scribner, Armstrong & Co., 1873.

Lloyd-Jones, Martyn. *Spiritual Depression: Its Causes and Cure.* Grand Rapids: Eerdmans, 1965.

Loane, Marcus. *They Were Pilgrims.* Edinburgh: Banner of Truth, 2006.

Lugioyo, Brian. *Martin Bucer's Doctrine of Justification: Reformation Theology and Early Irenicism.* Oxford Studies in Historical Theology. Oxford: Oxford University Press, 2010.

Luther, Martin. *Commentary on Saint Paul's Epistle to the Galatians.* Translated by Rev. Erasmus Middleton. Grand Rapids: Eerdmans, 1930.

M'Cheyne, Robert Murray. *Familiar Letters of the Rev. Robert Murray M'Cheyne: Containing an Account of His Travels as One of the Deputation Sent Out by the Church of Scotland on a Mission of Inquiry to the Jews in 1839.* Edited by Adam M'Cheyne. Robert Carter, 1849.

Macleod, Kenneth D. "Jonathan Edwards 7: Stockbridge and Princeton," Banner of Truth, March 16, 2007, https://banneroftruth.org/us/resources/articles/2007/jonathan-edwardssupsupbr7-stockbridge-and-princeton-1/.

Manton, Thomas. *An Exposition, with Notes, upon the Epistle of James.* In *The Complete Works of Thomas Manton.* Vol. 4. 1872. Reprint, Edinburgh: Banner of Truth, 2020.

Masefield, John. *Poems: Complete Edition with Recent Poems.* New York: Macmillan, 1974.

Mather, Cotton. *The Diary of Cotton Mather.* Vol. 2, *1709–1724.* New York: Frederick Ungar, 1911.

Melville, Herman. *Moby-Dick: Or the Whale.* New York: Tor Classics, 1996.

Mencken, Henry Louis. *A Mencken Chrestomathy.* 1949. Reprint, New York: Alfred A. Knopf, 1967.

Miller, Perry. *The New England Mind: From Colony to Province.* Cambridge, Mass.: Harvard University Press, 1953.

Murray, Iain H. *Jonathan Edwards: A New Biography.* Edinburgh: Banner of Truth, 1987.

———. *The Puritan Hope: A Study in Revival and the Interpretation of Prophecy.* Edinburgh: Banner of Truth, 1971.

Needham, Nick. *2000 Years of Christ's Power.* Vol. 4, *The Age of Religious Conflict.* Fearn, Scotland: Christian Focus Publications, 2016.

Newton, John. *The Works of John Newton.* Vol. 1. Edinburgh: Banner of Truth, 2015.

Orme, William. *Life and Times of the Rev. Richard Baxter with a Critical Examination of His Writings.* Vol. 1. Boston, Mass.: Crocker and Brewster, 1831.

Owen, John. "The Advantage of the Kingdom of Christ in the Shaking of the Kingdoms of the World." In *The Works of John Owen.* Vol. 8. Reprint, Edinburgh: Banner of Truth, 1967.

———. *Communion with God.* In *The Works of John Owen.* Vol. 2. Edinburgh: Banner of Truth, 1965.

———. *The Death of Death in the Death of Christ.* Reprint, Edinburgh: Banner of Truth, 1959.

———. *An Exposition upon Psalm CXXX.* In *The Works of John Owen.* Vol. 6. Edinburgh: Banner of Truth, 1966.

———. *Of the Mortification of Sin in Believers.* In *The Works of John Owen.* Vol. 6. Edinburgh: Banner of Truth, 1965.

———. *The Nature, Power, Deceit, and Prevalency of the Remainders of Indwelling Sin in Believers*. In *The Works of John Owen*. Vol. 6. Edinburgh: Banner of Truth, 1966.

Paton, John G. *Missionary to the New Hebrides: An Autobiography*. Edinburgh: Banner of Truth, 1994.

Perkins, William. *A Golden Chain*. In *The Works of William Perkins*. Vol. 6. Edited by Joel R. Beeke and Greg A. Salazar. Grand Rapids: Reformation Heritage Books, 2018.

"Prayer for the Sick and Spiritually Distressed—2." In *Liturgical Forms and Prayers of the United Reformed Churches in North America together with the Doctrinal Standards of URCNA*. Wellandport, Ontario: United Reformed Church in North America, 2018.

"Puritan Preface to the 1650 Psalter." The 1650 Psalter, accessed December 2, 2023. https://1650psalter.com/puritan-preface-to-the-1650-psalter/.

Rodigast, Samuel. "Whate'er My God Ordains Is Right, Holy His Will Abideth." Hymnary.org, accessed November 21, 2023. https://hymnary.org/text/whateer_my_god_ordains_is_right_holy_his.

Rutherford, Samuel. *Letters of Samuel Rutherford*. Edinburgh: Banner of Truth, 1981.

Sibbes, Richard. *Bowels Opened: Being Expository Sermons on Cant. IV. 16, V., VI*. In *Works of Richard Sibbes*. Vol. 2. Edited by Alexander B. Grosart. Reprint, Edinburgh: Banner of Truth, 1983.

———. *The Bruised Reed*. Rev. ed. Edinburgh: Banner of Truth, 1998.

Spickard, Paul R., and Kevin M. Cragg. *A Global History of Christians*. Grand Rapids: Baker Academic, 1994.

Spurgeon, Charles. "David Dancing before the Ark Because of His Election." Christian Classics Ethereal Library, accessed December 2, 2023. https://www.ccel.org/ccel/spurgeon/sermons34.xxix.html.

Stone, Jordan. *A Holy Minister: The Life and Spiritual Legacy of Robert Murray M'Cheyne*. Fearn, Scotland: Mentor, 2021.

Tanner, Jacob. "Cast Out by the World; Never Cast Out by Christ." G3 Ministries, July 15, 2022. https://g3min.org/cast-out-by-the-world-never-cast-out-by-christ/.

Tolkien, J. R. R. *The Fellowship of the Ring*. New York: Houghton Mifflin, 1993.

Trail, Robert. *Select Practical Writings*. Edinburgh: Banner of Truth, 2020.

Van Til, Cornelius. *Christian Apologetics*. 2nd ed. Edited by William Edgar. Phillipsburg, N.J.: P&R Publishing, 2003.

Watson, Thomas. *All Things for Good*. West Linn, Ore.: Monergism Books, 2020.

———. *A Body of Divinity*. Edinburgh: Banner of Truth, 1965; originally printed as *A Body of Practical Divinity*, 1692.

———. *Heaven Taken by Storm: Showing the Holy Violence a Christian Is to Put Forth in the Pursuit after Glory*. Grand Rapids: Soli Deo Gloria, 1992.

Whitefield, George. *Works*. Vol. 1. London: Edward and Charles Dilly, in the Poultry; and Messrs. Kincaid and Bell, at Edinburgh, 1771.

Whyte, Alexander. *Thomas Shepard: Pilgrim Father and Founder of Harvard*. 1909. Reprint, Grand Rapids: Reformation Heritage Books, 2007.

Willard, Samuel. *The Fountain Opened: or, The Great Gospel Priviledge of Having Christ Exhibited to Sinfull Men*. Boston, Mass.: B. Green and J. Allen, for Samuel Sewall Junior, 1700.

Yeaworth, David Victor. "Robert Murray M'Cheyne (1813–1843): A Study of an Early Nineteenth-Century Scottish Evangelical." PhD diss. University of Edinburgh, 1975.